D0722805

NATURE *into* ART

NATURE *into* ART

THE GARDENS *of* WAVE HILL

THOMAS CHRISTOPHER

photography by **NGOC MINH NGO**

Timber Press • Portland, Oregon

FRONTISPIECE

The leaves of upright wild ginger (*Saruma henryi*) are textured and shaped like hearts.

OPPOSITE

Stinking hellebore (*Helleborus foetidus*) brings flowers to the Wild Garden late in winter through early spring.

Copyright © 2019 by Thomas Christopher.
All rights reserved.

Published in 2019 by Timber Press, Inc.
All photographs by Ngoc Minh Ngo, except as noted on p. 288.

The Haseltine Building
133 S.W. Second Avenue, Suite 450
Portland, OR 97204-3527
timberpress.com

Printed in China

FSC
www.fsc.org

MIX
Paper from
responsible sources
FSC® C144853

Text and cover design by Hillary Caudle
Endpaper illustration by Kaitlin Pond

ISBN 978-1-60469-851-0
Catalog records for this book are available from the Library of Congress and the British Library.

This publication was made possible by the vision and support of one of Wave Hill's most ardent admirers, Beverly Frank. Throughout its creation, we were guided by consideration of her deep understanding of this extraordinary place. This book is for everyone who loves gardens, but it is especially for Beverly.

INTRODUCTION:
Wave Hill History and
Principles of Design   8

30

The Flower
Garden

56

The Gold
Border

70

The Monocot
and Aquatic
Gardens

166

The Herb and
Dry Gardens

186

Annual
Plantings

204

The Elliptical
Garden

90

The Shade
Border

116

The Wild
Garden

146

The Alpine
House and
Troughs

216

The
Conservatory

238

The Edges of
Everything

256

Wave Hill
Through the
Seasons

Further Reading   284

Acknowledgments   286

Photography Credits   288

Index   289

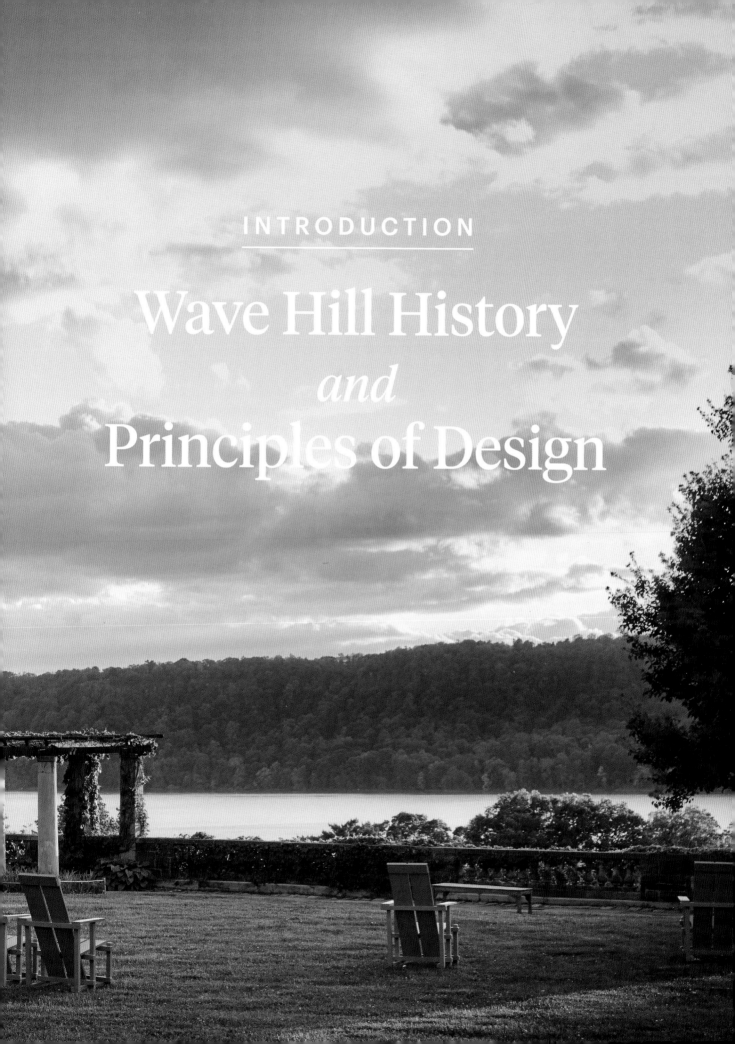

Wave Hill History
and
Principles of Design

PREVIOUS SPREAD

Located on 28 acres overlooking the
Hudson River, Wave Hill is one of the last
surviving country estates in New York
City's five boroughs.

BELOW

George W. Perkins, a financier who was
also instrumental in preserving the Hudson
River Palisades, assembled the current
Wave Hill property at the beginning of the
20th century.

From the first day Wave Hill opened to the public in 1967, this garden began to break new ground, figuratively as well as literally. It is no exaggeration to say that over the following decades Wave Hill remade American gardening—as it continues to do today.

The country had never seen a public garden like this: intimate, personal, rich, and dynamic. And Wave Hill remains unique. The gardeners there practice a kind of classic horticultural craftsmanship unrivaled among other public gardens in the United States. The skill and commitment to detail of the Wave Hill staff is legendary. Yet coupled with this devotion to the craft and its inherited lore is a design spirit that has always been, and continues to be, daring and innovative. Every year brings changes to Wave Hill, new combinations of colors, textures, and forms, new themes and experiments. The different areas of the garden, each an original composition in its own right, have become emblems of American gardening, yet all are undergoing continual redevelopment. For this reason, the Wave Hill way of gardening remains as timely and exciting today as it has ever been.

The site of the garden is unexpected and extraordinary. Wave Hill is one of the last surviving country estates in New York's five boroughs. Former farmland that became summer villas in the mid-19th century, this expanse of open space overlooking the Hudson River has, at various times, served as home to Mark Twain, Theodore Roosevelt, and Arturo Toscanini. As the residence of the British ambassador to the United Nations it even hosted Queen Elizabeth, the Queen Mother. In its present form, the 28-acre estate was assembled at the beginning of the 20th century from a couple of neighboring properties by its then-owner George W. Perkins, a financier who was also instrumental in preserving the Hudson River Palisades, the magnificent cliffs across the river from Wave Hill. Wave Hill as it looks today reflects a collaboration between Perkins and Viennese-trained landscape gardener Albert Millard to unify the two estates.

Louis Bauer, Wave Hill's current director of horticulture, and only its third, counts the site's location among its greatest assets. First, there is the surprise of passing through a gate in the Bronx and finding such a

A many-layered garden in May, with a dramatic backdrop.

rural retreat—in his words, "the vastness of the view and the generosity of the grounds." More important, though, from a grower's perspective, is the former estate's peculiar geography. Set on the crest of a steep slope, it is swept by the breezes blowing down and across the river valley below. These keep Wave Hill warmer in winter and cooler in summer and help to relieve the stagnant humidity that can grip New York City at midsummer.

Mark Twain wrote of the place, "I believe we have the noblest roaring blasts here I have ever known on land; they sing their hoarse song through the big tree-tops with a splendid energy that thrills me and stirs me and uplifts me and makes me want to live always." Certainly, the airy nature of the site benefits the longevity of many exotic plants; Wave Hill

Black cherry (*Prunus serotina*), left, and sweet gum (*Liquidambar styraciflua*), right, stand tall against the winds of Wave Hill so remarkable to Mark Twain.

Wave Hill House as it appeared in 1940.

Wave Hill's second estate house, Glyndor, in 1928.

can grow humidity-hating Mediterranean and South African plants outdoors that do not survive even in the botanical gardens elsewhere in the same city.

Aside from geography, however, some existing structures (including a pair of estate houses, Wave Hill House and Glyndor House, as they are now called), and a scattering of fine mature trees, there wasn't much planting here in 1967. George Perkins' heirs—the last private owners of the property—had donated the

TOP

A portrait of the Perkins family (date unknown), who donated Wave Hill to the City of New York in 1960.

ABOVE

The glasshouses as they were during the Perkins residency at Wave Hill; only the columned entrance (right) still survives in its original form.

RIGHT

Marco Polo Stufano (left) and John Nally (right) touring Wakehurst in West Sussex, England, managed by the Royal Botanic Gardens, Kew.

estate to the city in 1960, and other than periodic mowing of the grass, there had been little upkeep. The glasshouses that the Perkins family had built on the property were in a ruinous state, and though there were the remains of a rock garden, aquatic garden, pergola, and lower lawn, only a couple of shrubs survived. Even the rather straightforward, formal rose garden was in need of restoration.

The budget for the new public garden was not generous initially, but in some respects this was to prove a blessing. Founding director of horticulture Marco Polo Stufano and the three gardeners he was able to hire (the current staff includes seven gardeners, a horticulture assistant, and four interns, as well as an assistant director and director) were largely left to their own devices, though with limited funds for purchases. The plants for the new gardens they established had to be started on site, from seeds or cuttings. There is no better way to get to know a plant, and a willingness to start plants from scratch freed Wave Hill from dependence on local nurseries, which in the late 1960s were notably deficient in interesting plants, woody or herbaceous.

Indeed, the threadbare state of Wave Hill at its founding to some extent reflected the low ebb to which American horticulture as a whole had sunk. The great estates, together with their imported gardeners, which had once been the mainstay of fine gardening in the United States, had disappeared in the wake of World War II, leaving little other than suburban foundation plantings. To secure the kind of plants and design ideas to which Stufano aspired, it was necessary to go abroad. Repeated garden tours of Great Britain followed, as well as visits to Italy. Besides seeds and cuttings, what Stufano, and later his gardening partner John Nally, brought back from these trips was a very different approach to gardening.

Both men had backgrounds in the fine arts. Stufano had completed a degree in art history at Brown University (he had specialized in late-19th-century American architecture), and Nally had earned a master's degree in printmaking before signing on as a gardener at Wave Hill. For both of them, garden-making was as visceral as the work of an artist with a canvas and paints. They abhorred planning on paper and gardening by the rules of accepted plant combinations. Instead, taking a hint from the plantsmen's gardens they had visited in Great Britain, such as Christopher Lloyd's Great Dixter, Stufano and Nally relied on the plants to inspire them—with a personal twist, however.

For Stufano, the architecture of the plant, its form and pattern of growth, came first. Color was still essentially important, especially to Nally, as was texture and, where relevant, fragrance, but the displays were structured around architecture. Stufano and Nally would work out a design by setting out plants on the bed in question, arranging and re-arranging them on the spot. The color combinations that resulted were partly calculated, partly fortuitous; Stufano still maintains that some of his most striking combinations were inspired by accidental juxtapositions he observed in the nursery areas where he and his gardeners grew plants to a usable size.

These traditions survive at Wave Hill. Although Louis Bauer's experience with architectural studies and graphic arts makes him more comfortable with planning on paper, his design philosophy is unequivocal: "Plants first." For this reason, even in this era of ecologically defined gardens, Wave Hill remains an unashamed celebration of the special—sometimes rare and exotic, sometimes not—from all around the world. Stufano and Nally would bring back cuttings of choice plants spotted during their

OPPOSITE

From the start, the architecture of a plant was key—such as the structure of this weeping blue Atlas cedar (*Cedrus atlantica* 'Glauca Pendula') and the bronze fennel (*Foeniculum vulgare* 'Purpureum') at its foot.

ABOVE

A view of the Wild Garden through the weeping blue Atlas cedar. Ornamental onions (*Allium*) and camas (*Camassia*) in bloom.

far-flung travels. Closer to home, Nally was also the proud discoverer of the "Chicago Bus Stop" aster, a particularly fine specimen of the native heath aster (*Symphyotrichum ericoides*) that he pried from a crack in the sidewalk at the intersection of Chicago's Madison and Des Plaines Avenues.

Likewise, the plant combinations are all the more striking for breaking conventional rules concerning what goes with what. Stufano was very fond of what he called the Barbra Streisand effect, "a jarring combination of plants that initially sets your teeth on edge, but that you learn to appreciate not so much for its prettiness, but for its strength of character, its gutsiness." Louis Bauer and the current staff would also rather land on their faces occasionally than lapse into predictability. "Bury your mistakes" is one of their maxims, revealing both an impatience with the less than extraordinary and an understanding that there will be missteps while reaching for the novel delight.

The truth is, at Wave Hill, even the gardeners cannot anticipate the precise effects that the gardens will create each year. A theme that runs throughout the plantings is the self-sowing plants—foxgloves, larkspurs, aquilegias—that pop up throughout the landscape. In some areas, such as the Wild Garden, these self-sustaining performers play a greater role than in others, but with the exception of the Aquatic Garden, self seeders are always an element. These are edited by the gardeners, as a check on their numbers to keep them from overrunning less prolific neighbors, and to make sure that they enhance rather than compete with planned effects. Nevertheless, through these spontaneous seedlings, the garden expresses itself, adding an unforeseeable element to nearly all the displays.

Given the founders' aversion to master plans, it's no surprise that the landscape at Wave Hill grew organically and incrementally. Stufano's first major project was to renovate the glasshouses, creating spaces in which to cultivate the succulents and alpine plants that were among his passions, as well as a repository for the tropical plants that play such a big part in the summer displays. The late T.H. Everett, Stufano's mentor and an English-born horticulturist who ran the New York Botanical Garden (NYBG) when Stufano was a student there, called New York City's climate arctic in the winter and like Sumatra in the summer. He believed this weather prompts an exuberant growth that differentiates

OPPOSITE, CLOCKWISE FROM UPPER LEFT

Wave Hill remains an unashamed celebration of the special from all around the world, including *Idesia polycarpa*, a native of eastern Asia, in fall fruit; *Eucomis comosa* 'Sparkling Burgundy', like other *Eucomis* species from southern Africa, is dubbed pineapple lily because of its inflorescence; the foliage of redvein enkianthus (*Enkianthus campanulatus* 'Red Bells'), from Japan, turns a vibrant orange to crimson in fall; gladiolus (*Gladiolus* 'Carolina Primrose').

Wave Hill from the cooler, dimmer English gardens that played a role in its inspiration. In England, the plants tend to remain more compact. In New York, when plants are not cut back they soon exceed their bounds. But the heat, humidity, and intense sunlight are perfect for the tropical plants that come out of the Marco Polo Stufano Conservatory to ornament the open-air gardens during the warmer months, adding a flamboyance that is very un-English and thoroughly New York.

After the glasshouses were rebuilt, the creation of individual gardens began. Perhaps subconsciously, Stufano and Nally recognized that the sweeping view across the Hudson River to the monumental Palisades

OPPOSITE, CLOCKWISE FROM TOP LEFT

Enthusiastic self sowers that pop up every year at Wave Hill include columbine (*Aquilegia* species); poppies (*Papaver somniferum*); foxglove (*Digitalis* species); and love-in-a-mist (*Nigella damascena*).

Marco Polo Stufano's first major project was to replace the glasshouses; the entrance to the Perkins' structure was preserved and incorporated into the new glasshouses.

Rebuilding the glasshouses.

cliffs was an asset that needed to be rationed lest it overwhelm their plantings. Aside, then, from a pergola-ornamented overlook where the sweep is fully exploited, the views are carefully controlled. In another early project they undertook, for example, the conversion of the old rock garden to the informal and eclectic Wild Garden, the entry is at the garden's lower end and the visitor's attention is kept facing uphill, away from the river, on the splendid tousled beds and meandering paths, until the gazebo at the upper end is reached. Only after entering the gazebo and looking out through the frame of a pair of carefully clipped, mounded yews is one allowed a view of the river and opposing cliffs.

This garden area was just the first of many to be developed, each conceived on an intimate, human scale, their growth organic and often opportunistic. The old rose garden was torn out and the rectilinear space it had occupied was transformed into the Flower Garden, a series of beds in which Nally explored the contrasts and harmonies between different perennials and annuals. A swimming pool was filled in and is the center of a formal display of native plants (the Elliptical Garden). Just as often, though, it was the nature of the site that inspired the design. The canopy of mature trees at the northern end of the cultivated area inspired a shade border, and the stepped footprint of former glasshouses became a pair of south-facing terraces, comprising a dry garden and an herb garden. (Eight of the property's 28 acres are woodland, officially the Herbert and Hyonja Abrons Woodland.)

Although decisions ostensibly rested with Stufano, he recalls the designing of the gardens as often a process of argument. John Nally and later John Emanuel, another creative and influential voice on the horticultural staff, argued energetically with Stufano, who remembers at least one occasion when the two overrode his diktat. There were two parrotia trees growing in the nursery and Stufano had chosen a planting spot for one of them, ordering the other one to

OPPOSITE

The new conservatory provides a winter-time refuge for the tropical plants that play a pivotal part in Wave Hill's summer displays.

BELOW

The entrance to the Wild Garden is arranged to keep the visitor facing upward and away from the river view.

be discarded. But he recalls with affection and amusement how he later discovered the second parrotia occupying another spot inside the garden: Nally and Emmanuel had decided on their own to rescue it. Wide latitude was also allowed Nally in arranging and refining the Flower Garden; Emmanuel took charge of the Wild Garden as it continued to grow and develop.

This is a process that has expanded under Louis Bauer's supervision. He has allowed the gardeners all to specialize, each one concentrating mainly on a particular area of the garden. A crucial factor in making this work has been the fact that as a group, the gardeners have an intimate knowledge of the grounds as a whole, thanks to an exceptional degree of stability in the staff. Most of the gardeners have worked at Wave Hill for many years and learned their horticulture there, often starting as interns. This was a necessity in Stufano's day, as expert gardeners were scarce in the United States when he started at Wave Hill, and he was obliged to train his own. Even Bauer learned much of his gardening this way, working as a gardener under Stufano's direction for a decade before leaving Wave Hill to serve as the director of horticulture at Greenwood Gardens in New Jersey, another historic estate, for ten years.

Bauer's return to Wave Hill in 2013 was a homecoming, and part of his role today is to serve as institutional memory. While the gardeners experiment with new arrangements, Bauer remembers what has been tried in the past, what worked and what didn't. He knows which of the self-seeders have proven aggressive, and which will overrun choice but less robust neighbors if not severely restrained. He knows that the Flower Garden isn't the first of Wave Hill's gardens to bloom in spring, because the space that the very early, ephemeral spring flowers would occupy is needed for plants that bloom later in the season. Such continuity is important. Before being taken over by gardener Gelene Scarborough in 2014, the Wild Garden had, atypically, passed through the hands of three different gardeners in five years and, as Bauer admits, "it showed." Because the gardeners hadn't had time to learn the garden, they didn't have the knowledge of what to restrain. The more delicate elements of the garden's palette were being lost.

This succession of bloom, incidentally, is one of the areas in which the Wave Hill gardeners best demonstrate their mastery. The conventional wisdom, of course, is that a garden should have something in bloom, or

OPPOSITE

Only as you enter the gazebo at the Wild Garden's upper end, and turn around, do you have an opportunity to focus on the view of the river and contrasting Palisades cliffs.

OPPOSITE, TOP

Views change with the seasons: a sugar
maple (*Acer saccharum*), rear right, and an
American elm (*Ulmus americana*) furnish
a summertime backdrop for a bottlebrush
buckeye (*Aesculus parviflora*), center front,
and a variegated giant dogwood (*Cornus
controversa* 'Variegata'), left front.

OPPOSITE, BOTTOM

In the same scene, winter strips away the
foliage, revealing the intrinsic structures of
the trees and shrubs.

at least in color, during every season. This is to an extent true of Wave Hill; in early spring, for example, the Alpine House and the Wild Garden are glorious, and the woodland flowers of the Shade Border move to center stage later in that season. Other gardens offer displays throughout the summer and fall, and winter visits to Wave Hill, when the skeletons of the shrubs and trees are exposed, are well worth the trip.

There is also a recognition of the realities of the New York City climate, however, and of the habits of visitors. Spring is relatively short in New York, soon overtaken by heat and drought as summer settles in with the arrival of June. Summer is torrid, and though there is much that can be done with tropicals during that season, even Wave Hill's most faithful supporters tend to stay at home and indoors some days. Fall, by contrast, is a long and glorious season of sunny days and cool but not yet cold nights. That is a season when, by design, Wave Hill's gardens peak, when all its patrons are eager to catch the last good weather of the year.

To time the garden this way is a point of pride as well as a service to the visitors. It's easy to have a garden that is glorious in spring what with that season's profuse bloomers, such as peonies, lilacs, and tulips. It takes real skill, though, to have the garden peak again in the fall. There is much preparation—early staking and grooming—involved in making sure that plantings will hold up through the summer and beyond. The tendency to overplant spring flowers must also be avoided. Space must be left for the insertion of fall bloomers such as asters. Careful timing is also essential: in late June and early July, the reseeders are edited and thinned to make room for a late planting of dahlias, tender salvias, and gladioli that come into flower as the days grow shorter.

Marco Polo Stufano is clear that Wave Hill is now Louis Bauer's garden, and has embraced the idea that it must continue to change. One innovation, subtle though important, is the work that Bauer is doing to improve access. Assembled as it was, originally, from two separate properties, Wave Hill continues to deal with some disconnects between different areas of the grounds, and ADA accessibility is less than ideal. These will be improved. More significantly from a horticultural point of view, some of Stufano's plantings have aged out. Dwarf conifers, for example, though very slow-growing, can eventually attain a considerable size, and some that were planted in the Wild Garden have had half a century to outgrow their space. The result was a garden that increasingly looked like a

conifer collection. The outsized plants have been removed and replaced, often with more recent cultivars of the same species that do not grow as large, sometimes with other plants favored by the current gardeners.

On one score, though, the gardeners of Wave Hill past and present are united. Despite having created such a crowd-pleaser, they have worked primarily to satisfy themselves.

"In making a garden," says Stufano, "we never did anything we thought people would like. We did what we thought was the right thing to do." Ironically, this willingness to break with accepted practice has been crucial to Wave Hill's success. Inspiration from European traditions was brought home and then translated to an American idiom. Direction was taken from the site and from the plants. Rules were broken and remade. In the process, an example of originality and creativity was created that visitors and colleagues can take home and apply to their own landscapes.

All in all, the effect is more than ever what Mark Twain described a century ago: Wave Hill has the power to thrill, stir and uplift, to make the visitor feel more alive.

OPPOSITE

A burst of blue asters contributes to the fall display that is such an important part of Wave Hill's year.

BELOW

April is a time of awakening: willows brighten; almonds, cherries, and bulbs come into bloom, and the lawns turn green, creating a vivid contrast with the shrubby dogwood, *Cornus sanguinea* 'Midwinter Fire'.

The Flower Garden

PREVIOUS SPREAD

View of the Flower Garden from the
northeast.

OPPOSITE

The "$16.30 Garden" that Marco Polo
Stufano and John Nally grew from seed.
The original budget for plants was small.

e can't do that here."

Marco Polo Stufano was told this over and over again by
both visitors and accomplished gardeners when he returned in 1967
from his first tour of English gardens, full of memories of the colorful
and subtle mixed borders that adorned those landscapes. Such linear
complexes of perennials, annuals, and shrubs presented a unique vision
of living colors blended and contrasted, and Stufano, as a student of art
as well as a horticulturist, was fascinated.

Encouraged by Miss Elizabeth Hall, the recently retired head librarian
of the New York Botanical Garden and a leading light of the New York
horticultural scene, Stufano was buying and reading books. Not just
English gardening books, but also American classics by authors such
as Louise Beebe Wilder and Richardson Wright, whose descriptions
indicated that a far more sophisticated approach to flower colors had
once held sway on this side of the Atlantic, too. By the 1960s, however,
American flower gardening had devolved into simplistic patterns of
annuals in primary colors. Stufano rebelled.

First he, then later he and John Nally when Nally joined the staff in
the early 1970s, decided to indeed "do that here"—just with different
plants. A simple resolution, but it had to wait for Stufano and Nally's
impatience with Wave Hill's rose garden to reach the boiling point. A
holdover from Wave Hill's days as a private estate, the rose garden was
a simple arrangement of eight rectangular beds framed by four long,
L-shaped borders, occupying altogether a 70-by-90-foot expanse. The
turf paths that divided the beds were narrow and could not stand up
to the traffic of a public garden. Nor was it a good spot for growing
sun-hungry roses, given the shade of a large old elm situated outside the

garden's southwest corner. The shrub and hybrid tea roses in the beds required constant spraying and upkeep, and the return on all that work was but scrawny growth. They had to go, Stufano decided. Nally agreed.

Getting the City of New York to broaden the paths and repave them with brick and bluestone was a slow process. In the meantime, just to show what could be done, Stufano and Nally for three years planted a "$16.30 Garden" of annuals they raised from seeds purchased from a catalog for that exact amount. This was one of the pair's early encounters with self-seeding flowers. So many of the annuals in the former rose beds returned as volunteer seedlings that, Stufano jokes, they could have called the composition the $14.20 Garden the second year, and in the third year, they could have been turning a profit with the sale of seedlings. This lesson was not forgotten, as self-seeding flowers came to be a mainstay not just of the Flower Garden but of Wave Hill's gardens in general. With the annuals, Stufano and Nally also began to develop the soft and undulating style of planting that would become a hallmark of Wave Hill.

OPPOSITE

The Marco Polo Stufano Conservatory provides a backdrop for the Flower Garden.

BELOW

Backlit by the early morning light, the Flower Garden offers a lush interplay of textures, forms, and colors.

Once the new, broader, and more durable paths were finally installed, Stufano and Nally set about creating what they called, in a bow to the vintage garden books Stufano had been absorbing, an "old-fashioned flower garden." Originally planted with such traditional favorites as clematises, irises, and peonies, the concept soon succumbed to the duo's omnivorous appetite for fine plants and evolved into something far less predictable. Today, the only requirements for inclusion are outstanding form and color, so that exceptional cultivars of garden standbys are placed alongside exotic imports, with the effect of a sort of brilliantly eclectic cottage garden.

In the conversion, the basic layout of the rose garden's beds was preserved, as was the rustic cedar fence that surrounded the space. Even a handful of climbing roses were retained: those that shade the benches set into the fence on the east and west sides of the garden are original and now 60 to 80 years old. For the rest though, the space was transformed, becoming a sort of master class in garden color, taught with an innovative flair.

Each bed had a theme: the extreme northeastern plot was the red bed, where plants with red flowers and foliage predominated. Adjacent to it was the plum bed, where purples were the dominant hue. Over the years, the color palette has evolved and changed as the gardeners have changed. The plum bed, for example, under the care of Harnek Singh, the current gardener in the Flower Garden, has morphed into an intriguing, if unconventional, mixture of magentas, deep pinks, and oranges. Yet the original concept, of each bed devoted to a contrasting or harmonious color palette, has persisted. There is, currently, a bed of pink, peach, and orange; a bed of yellow foliages accented with pink flowers; a silver bed, where elements of pale yellow and blue provide contrast; a blue bed, with accents of white and yellow; and a white bed. The outer, framing beds, have been planted to echo adjacent inner beds.

Old-fashioned beauties such as irises, peonies, and clematises recall the Flower Garden's original incarnation. Biennials such as foxgloves are dropped into vacant spots in fall and removed after they finish blooming in July.

OPPOSITE, CLOCKWISE FROM TOP LEFT

Vintage flowers: the non-climbing solitary clematis (Clematis integrifolia); a peony cultivar; Clematis ×triternata 'Rubromarginata'; a survivor from Wave Hill's original rose garden, 'Silver Moon'.

Given Stufano's academic background in the history of architecture, it should not be surprising that the beds are strongly structured. There was the precise geometry of the whole, of course, but each bed is also anchored by some sort of structural element, either architectural or natural. A pollarded golden catalpa tree, for instance, a dome of bold yellow foliage, serves as the focal point of the yellow bed. An heirloom violet-blossomed climbing rose, 'Veilchenblau', anchors the plum bed—and when the rose passes out of bloom, similarly colored clematis flowers take over. This tradition has been maintained and extended, with a quartet of eight-foot-tall, obelisk-shaped tuteurs, painted the same pale blue as the entryway of the adjacent conservatory, framing the center of the garden. Remove these focal points, and the expanses of flowers would be flat, both literally and figuratively.

Red-gold blossoms give the rose 'Alchymist' (introduced in 1956) its name. Here it clambers up one of the Flower Garden's tuteurs.

ABOVE LEFT

Another survivor from the original rose garden is this 1924 climber, 'Mary Wallace', which clothes the arbor overhanging a bench.

OPPOSITE

Iris sibirica 'Lady Vanessa'

Dahlia 'Bednall Beauty' (lower left) ignites the red bed, uniting with scarlet *Sanguisorba officinalis* (center) and *Salvia* 'Royal Bumble' (right), playing off the blossoms of golden lace, *Patrinia scboisifolia* 'Nagoya' (center), foliage of smokebush, *Cotinus coggygria* 'Royal Purple' (upper left), and *Prunus cerasifera* 'Atropurpurea'.

In the plum bed, a rustic tuteur provides structure and a lift for rose 'Veilchenblau'.

Steely blue sea holly (*Eryngium planum*), left, harmonizes with the clear blue of giant larkspur (*Consolida ajacis*) in the blue bed.

Form plays as important a role as color, even in the Flower Garden. Here the jagged foliage and thistlelike blossoms of cardoon (*Cynara cardunculus*), lower center, contrast with the glaucous leaves and yellow, daisylike blossoms of the large coneflower (*Rudbeckia maxima*), upper right, and the pale blue, starburst flowerheads of African lily (*Agapanthus africanus*), upper left.

Canna 'Phasion' TROPICANNA (left) adds a flamboyant note to the orange bed, harmonizing with the more delicate shades of 'Classic Elise' and 'Robin Hood' dahlias.

Siberian iris (*Iris sibirica* 'Pansy Purple') furnishes a rich purple note in the blue bed.

Architectural elements structure the Flower Garden beds while contributing a rhythmic punctuation to the planting as a whole.

There are harmonies aplenty here. In the red bed, for example, the dusky crimson flowers of a sweet William, *Dianthus barbatus* 'Heart Attack', play well with a purplish-leaved heuchera and the wine-colored *Eucomis comosa* 'Sparkling Burgundy'. But there are also contrasts, even clashes, because the gardeners of Wave Hill have never been afraid to break the rules of conventional design in their pursuit of the memorable and exceptional. So, for example, purples are juxtaposed with oranges, and pinks with yellows.

The two latter pairings are frowned upon in the gardening literature, but forget the rules is the message of this garden. Please yourself. Marco Polo Stufano's advice to those who feel insecure about their handling of color is to spend time at art museums, identifying what pleases you. And while there, dip into other, non-Western traditions. Look at the remarkable and (by American standards) unconventional color themes of Chinese porcelains and textiles. Study Indian paintings, with their vibrant, often clashing hues.

Initially, many of the more unusual plants came from England, often as seeds or cuttings brought back in Stufano or Nally's luggage. Many of these imports didn't pan out, not being able to withstand the combined heat and humidity of New York summers. After toting back starts of desirable but less-hardy cultivars of *Phygelius* (Cape fuchsia), for example, Marco finally admitted that they wouldn't perform as shrubs in the Bronx and largely gave up on them. (This plant was later reintroduced and grown successfully as an herbaceous perennial.) Other imports flourished, however. Stufano and Nally picked some ripe seed of *Verbena bonariensis* from a plant at the famous English garden Great Dixter, and not only did it survive at Wave Hill, it provided a steady supply of its

LEFT TO RIGHT

A tuteur supplies a needed third dimension to a sea of perennials, as well as serving as a trellis for a climbing rose; a hollyhock (*Alcea rosea*) finds support in a more rustic structure; Helen of Troy foxglove (*Digitalis trojana*) furnishes upright spires. Verticals bring a third dimension to the garden.

Harmonies and counterpoints are central to the
Flower Garden's display.

own seed that the gardeners could share with admiring visitors. Though he had to disapprove, Marco took it as a sign of success when visitors to his garden started to beg for cuttings.

As the American nursery industry became more adventurous, unusual plants were obtained closer to home. The Flower Garden wasn't just about rarities, though; a common plant with uncommon beauty has always been welcome there. Harnek Singh, for example, has splashed a variegated euonymus, a meat-and-potatoes plant as he describes it, a standby of suburban landscaping, into the yellow bed. It's the right plant in the right spot, brightening the shady bed just as effectively as its neighbor, a variegated masterwort (*Peucedanum ostruthium* 'Daphnis') introduced from France, and harmonizing nicely with a Japanese forest grass, *Hakonechloa macra* 'All Gold'. It isn't novelty, per se, that attracts Singh. On the contrary, he says that he rarely tries a new plant until he has seen it in some other garden and had a chance to evaluate its qualities in the flesh.

By design, this garden has a remarkable flexibility and chameleon-like ability to take on the personality of its current caretaker. Perhaps only 30 percent of the plants in the garden, according to Singh, are shrubs or perennials. The rest are either the reseeding annuals that provide the changeable, seasonal background, biennials, or perennials grown as biennials. These are started from seed in cell packs in mid- to late July and overwintered in four- or six-inch pots in a cold frame outdoors. Many of the biennials, such as foxgloves (*Digitalis* species), are dropped into the garden in late fall as fading plants open up spots. These are then removed after they finish blooming to make room, in turn, for the dahlia tubers, gladiolus corms, and tender salvias that are planted in mid- to late June to provide late summer and fall color. Excess volunteer seedlings are rescued and moved temporarily to pots, to be dropped back into the garden if a hole should appear.

Although not the shrub that it makes in warmer climates, the species-type Cape fuchsia (*Phygelius capensis*) does grow as an herbaceous perennial at Wave Hill—unlike the less hardy cultivars.

The speckled flowers of a martagon lily seem to glow when set against the yellow-green leaves of *Catalpa bignonioides* 'Aurea'.

The Flower Garden

The paler hues of *Dahlia*
'Daydreamer' play off
darker shades in the
peach-colored group.

Singh agrees that much of what he does, removing and replacing plants, could be defined as horticultural choreography. Swapping plants in and out changes not only the sequence of flowering, but the character of the bloom. For example, 2017 in the Flower Garden was jokingly declared The Year of the Umbel, because of the wealth of parasol-bloomed plantings that year. These included *Ammi majus* (bishop's weed, a more refined look-alike for Queen Anne's lace); *Ammi visnaga* (similar to but stockier than *A. majus*); and a wild carrot with a burgundy-colored flowerhead, *Daucus carota* 'Dara'.

Successful choreography depends on careful planning. Singh works out the colors of the garden and the drop-in plants a year ahead of time, using his phone to post notes to the cloud when thoughts occur to him. (He also keeps notes on plants and combinations that aren't working.) As an enthusiastic sampler of gardens here and abroad, he takes photographs while on visits. These he organizes into folders, also on his phone and in the cloud. Sometimes what he draws from the photographs are concepts and effects, sometimes specific plants. *Lonicera periclymenum* 'Graham Thomas', a yellow-flowered honeysuckle that Singh noted on a visit to Nymans, the celebrated National Trust garden in Southeast England, went straight from his phone to a tripod of poles in the yellow bed, helping to lend the garden better structure.

Another way that those in charge of the Flower Garden have cultivated flexibility is to grow specimens in pots and, when the plants are at

OPPOSITE

Gutsy contrasts, such as this clash of purple (*Salvia guaranitica* 'Amistad') with a bold orange (*Dahlia* 'Japanese Bishop'), add punch to the Flower Garden.

BELOW, LEFT TO RIGHT

Part of the Year of the Umbel in 2017: masterwort (*Peucedanum ostruthium* 'Daphnis') contributes its parasol-like flowerheads to the Flower Garden.

Bishop's weed (*Ammi majus*), front, with ox-eye sunflower (*Heliopsis helianthoides* 'Prairie Sunset'), left, and butterfly bush (*Buddleja davidii* 'Fortune'), right.

Bishop's weed (rear) with 'Pink Delight' butterfly bush (front center), and poppy seed capsules (front right).

Queen Anne's lace (*Daucus carota* 'Dara').

their peak, insert them into the garden, pairing them with in-ground plants to create partnerships that complement both. A bowl of orange nasturtiums is juxtaposed with pale purple irises, electrifying each. Or a more soothing note may be struck, as in the very center of the garden, where a stone rondel might serve in spring as a setting for a pot of apricot wallflowers (*Erysimum* 'Apricot Sunset') lounging next to the apricot-touched yellow flowers of *Tulipa batalinii* 'Bright Gem'. Later in the growing season, the same site might host a pairing of New Zealand flax (*Phormium tenax*) 'Jester', with its red and rusty orange leaves, and the appropriately named California poppy (*Eschscholzia californica*) 'Copper Pot'.

Clematis tibetana embraces a panicle hydrangea (*Hydrangea paniculata*) in an autumn scene at the entrance to the Flower Garden.

OPPOSITE

The aptly named California poppy (*Eschscholzia californica*) 'Copper Pot'.

Often, containers are used to inject structure. Agaves were Singh's first love in gardening and he is also responsible for the succulent house in Wave Hill's conservatory. These highly architectural plants are often moved out to the Flower Garden during warmer weather, to create contrasts of form that complement the contrasts of color.

Creating a succession of blooms is generally understood as a means for keeping a garden in flower, but it is also a strategy for keeping the colors of the garden in step with the seasons. Spring light is delicate and spring bloomers tend to be the same, lending themselves to harmonies and more delicate, pastel effects. By the time late summer and fall arrive, with their intense light, the bolder the combination, the better. "By fall," Louis Bauer says, "the volume of everything has become so big, I think color has to be a little stronger to keep up. . . . In very small ways, springtime can have some bold color, but it's always a little more pure and petite. It's never so overblown and complex as in the fall."

But Bauer recommends an adventurous spirit in general. "Be bold, try anything, try everything. Don't be limited by what you hear works well.

Ornamental sages, such as this *Salvia* 'Waverly', are essential elements of the fall display.

RIGHT

Autumn in Wave Hill's Flower Garden.

Look around and see what *you* like." And don't think too much about it, he urges. Keep the garden flexible, as the Wave Hill gardeners have done. Most of the Flower Garden's color comes from perennials and self-seeding biennials, with some annuals dropped in seasonally. Everything is moveable. If it doesn't work, move it.

Perhaps Stufano puts it best. "My thought on color was always, do what pleases you personally. If I hate your garden, I don't have to come look at it."

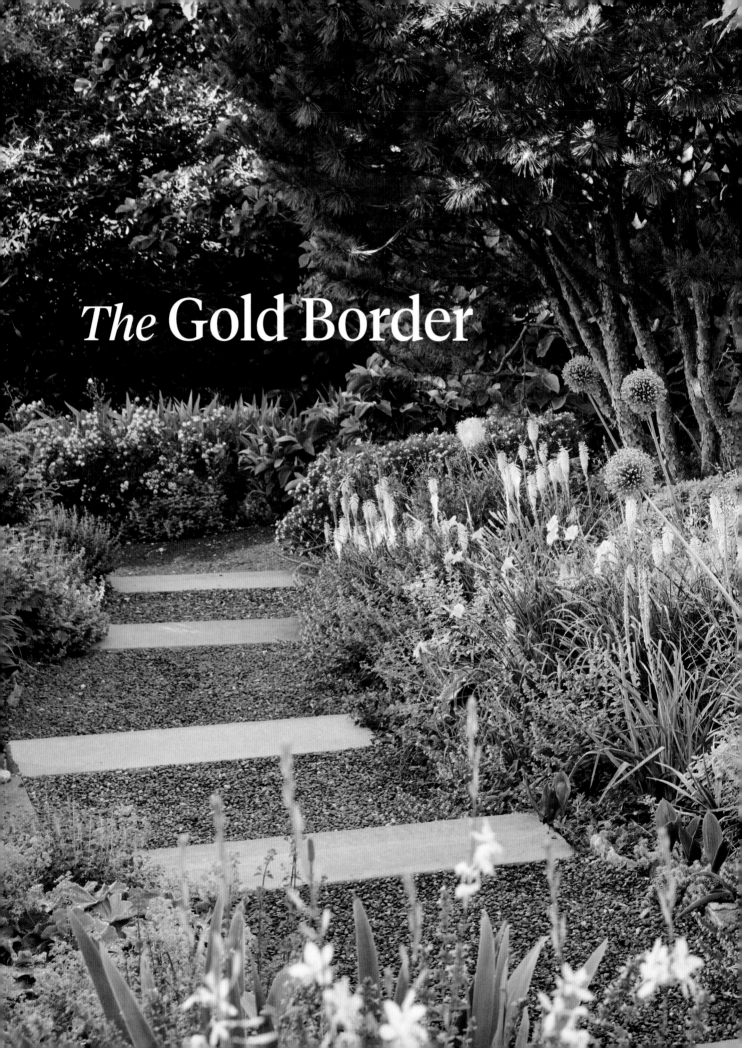

The Gold Border

PREVIOUS SPREAD

A native golden hoptree (*Ptelea trifoliata* 'Aurea') shows off its rounded form, harmonizing with the spherical allium seed heads that punctuate a rivulet of torch lilies (*Kniphofia uvaria* 'Echo Yellow').

"Monochromatic" may sound suspiciously similar to "monotonous." In fact, though, as this area of Wave Hill proves, a garden tuned to one hue can make a dynamic, even exciting, horticultural statement.

Such a planting offers advantages. For the gardener who is struggling with design, it provides an intrinsically harmonious display; because its colors are all related, they blend naturally and effortlessly. Yet if this type of display is well suited to the struggling gardener, it also offers a fine field for the display of the expert's sophisticated plantsmanship. In particular, the single-hue garden, by eliminating from the landscape the easy drama of color contrasts, calls for greater skill in the handling of two particular aspects, plant form and texture. At the same time, it enhances their impact, enabling a more acute pleasure in these two often-overlooked plant features.

HISTORY OF THE SINGLE-HUED GARDEN

Without question, the most famous example of a monochromatic garden is the White Garden Vita Sackville-West created as part of her larger garden at Sissinghurst Castle in southeast England. A masterful demonstration of horticultural finesse, the drama of the white garden is only enhanced by its lack of other colors. Conceived as an outdoor room, the garden is heavily architectural, with rectilinear brick paths and fastidiously clipped hedges of yew and box. Within the rectangular spaces these features created, Sackville-West installed luxurious, romantic tangles of white flowers and silver and green foliage. To colorize such a composition would only distract and diminish its impact.

The Gold Border

Across the Atlantic, Louise Beebe Wilder, the most popular American garden writer of her day, also took up the subject of color-themed gardens in her 1918 book *Colour in My Garden*. In a chapter titled "Flowers of Light," she wrote, "As I have said many times I am not fond of gardens or borders devoted to one colour; but if ever I were tempted to make one it would be yellow in all the frank and pleasant tones from cream and buff and the bright butter yellows through apricot to the tawny ochreous shades, reaching now and then to flame."

The language may be dated but the information is not. Though upper-class by background, Wilder was a hands-on gardener. In fact, the garden club she founded was "The Working Gardeners of Bronxville" and that was precisely what she was, for Wilder personally installed and maintained her one-acre garden in that New York suburb. She took pride in the fact that her writings were drawn from first-hand experience rather than theorizing.

THE GOLD BORDER AT WAVE HILL

In addition to the historical precedents, there is also a very practical reason for the creation of a gold border such as the one at Wave Hill. Plants with golden-hued or golden-variegated leaves can be difficult to work into the garden at large. They tend to obtrude. That is, long habituation has taught the eye that plant foliage ought to be green, with the result that golden foliage practically shouts its individuality. Golden-variegated foliage, with its bicolored striping or mottling, is perhaps even more eye-catching. In either case, plants with such luminous leaves automatically jump to the fore as focal points. This can be useful when it is the effect you want, but awkward when your desire is for foliage to blend into the surroundings. The problem is heightened when the impact is as subtle as it often is at Wave Hill, and certainly unacceptable in a more naturalistic setting, such as the Wild Garden, adjacent to the Gold Border.

Yet there are many fine, even extraordinary, golden-foliaged plants. And the gardeners at Wave Hill have never been ones to resist extraordinary plants. A gold border creates an opportunity to play with these in a distinct setting where they will not distract from their green-leaved fellows.

As it happened, though, the Gold Border at Wave Hill was not the result of a deliberate plan. Instead, it grew organically. There was a secluded spot, a slope, enclosed by trees and shrubbery and therefore somewhat visually isolated, that connected the Wild Garden and Aquatic Garden with the Perkins Visitor Center. At the head of a stairway that climbs the steepest part of this slope stood a large eastern arborvitae whose new foliage had a yellowish cast when it emerged in spring. (Though typically described as a dwarf variant of the species, this specimen 'Globosa' eastern arborvitae demonstrates a characteristic common among such dwarf evergreens; many are not intrinsically dwarf but merely very slow growing. This venerable specimen at Wave Hill now stands approximately 20 feet tall and 15 feet wide.) Marking the bottom of this slope, roughly 45 feet from the arborvitae, was an equally remarkable dwarf Japanese red pine, *Pinus densiflora* 'Umbraculifera'. The latter tree, a multi-trunked, umbrella-like specimen, has dark-green foliage which contrasts nicely with its cinnamon-colored bark.

This recommended the site as a place to experiment with other golden-hued plants. Sometime around the mid-1970s, as Marco Polo Stufano remembers it, he and John Nally began locating choice golden-foliaged shrubs and perennials there.

In creating a monochromatic garden, the designer faces a special challenge: the more typical garden relies on contrasts of foliage and flower colors as its principal source of drama. There are color contrasts in the monochromatic garden, of course, but they are subtler. The needles of a Japanese false cypress (*Chamaecyparis pisifera* 'Filifera Aurea') and the flowers of a daylily (*Hemerocallis* 'Golden Chimes') may both be described as golden ("aurea" means golden in Latin), but juxtapose the two and you will notice that the daylily blossoms are a rich, buttery gold while the conifer has a greenish tinge to its yellow. Such juxtapositions can lend character and richness to the border, but don't spark real excitement. For bolder drama, the designer of a monochromatic garden must rely on contrasts and harmonies of texture and form.

That may sound challenging, but in fact it agreed very well with Stufano's predilections. He has always felt that one must begin the design of a planting by building it architecturally, asserting that form and shape are the most important things, and color comes after.

OPPOSITE

The head of the Gold Border is punctuated by a Japanese false cypress (*Chamaecyparis pisifera* 'Filifera Aurea') and an eastern arborvitae (*Thuja occidentalis* 'Globosa') to the rear, with two of the shrubs that provide the backbone of the border, a lilac daphne (*Daphne genkwa*) and a variegated euonymus (*Euonymus fortunei* 'Emerald 'n' Gold') in the foreground.

"You build it architecturally to begin with and then you see what you have in the color range that you want to use," he says. Building it architecturally translates into concentrating on the shape of the plants and how they relate to each other, which he believes is important in any part of the garden—the verticals, the spreading things, the low things, the high things, and putting them all together in an arrangement. Only when you have established this do you worry specifically about colors.

The rhythmic repetition of shrubs at the back of the Gold Border echoes the rhythm of the adjoining steps.

Louis Bauer expresses this in explicitly theatrical terms. He points to the larger specimens that serve as the frame for this feature: the eastern arborvitae and the Japanese red pine, and behind the border, a 150-year-old sugar maple and a 200-year-old elm. "These are all part of a picture," he contends, "the architectural framing of the Gold Border. They make the stage. They are the proscenium."

Bauer differentiates form from architecture, though, believing that form is one scale down. He compares the euphorbias and kniphofias with their fine linear, vertically oriented foliage, to the horizontally oriented, small leaves of a creeping evergreen euonymous (*Euonymus fortunei* 'Emerald 'n' Gold'). Together they make a contrast that is not quite architecture but is more about texture and upright versus horizontal shapes. Such contrasts of architecture, form, and texture obviously assume a greater importance in a planting where contrasts of colors are subdued.

As for the wisdom of including a Japanese barberry (*Berberis thunbergii*), widely decried as an invasive plant, Bauer notes that the cultivar in the Gold Border, *Berberis thunbergii* 'Aurea', produces little fruit and is not invasive. He agrees, however, that the species type of this shrub is a prolific fruit-bearer, and has been spread by birds far outside its original garden settings.

There is a cycle in this border. Originally, it was planted largely with shrubs, to reduce the labor required to maintain it. There were perennials, too, but they were largely crowded out as the shrubs expanded. Over the last couple of years, though, Albert Cabrera, the gardener responsible for the Gold Border, has removed some of the overgrown shrubs and enthusiastically replanted perennials. These now dominate the display, at least during their period of bloom.

The perennials serve not only to reinforce the effect of the shrubs, but also as a counterpoint. Many of them bloom in shades of yellow or gold, echoing the gold and gold-variegated shrubs. But a scattering of others bloom in colors deliberately chosen for the strength of their contrast to gold and yellow. Purple, as in the flowers of the *Allium* 'Early Emperor' or the grape hyacinth *Muscari latifolia*, is the complementary contrast of yellow, and the resulting color clash makes the yellows that surround these plants seem more vibrant. Blue, as in the flowers of the *Pulmonaria* 'Diana Clare', is the complementary contrast of gold and has a similar effect on the border's gold foliages and flowers.

Pheasant-eye narcissus (*Narcissus poeticus* cultivar) in the Gold Border.

The colors of the perennials change, naturally, with the progress of the seasons. Subtler but still significant is the shift in foliage colors. Generally, the yellow foliages are brighter when they first emerge in spring, becoming more subdued, and commonly greener, as summer settles in. Autumn brings a refreshing of foliage hues, as the leaves of some of the woody plants such as the golden hoptree, the *Ptelea trifoliata* 'Aurea', return to yellow, harmonizing attractively with the vivid red fruits of the tea viburnum (*Viburnum setigerum*).

It's the color of the blossoms that grabs visitors' attention, but even with these flowers, form is important. It's worth noting that the Dutch landscape designer Piet Oudolf (designer of New York's High Line

ABOVE

The stately, globular flowerheads of *Allium* 'Early Emperor' dominate the border when in peak bloom, furnishing an enlivening contrast to gold-themed perennials and shrubs.

OPPOSITE

A view of the Gold Border in full spring display with the umbrella form of the Japanese red pine (*Pinus densiflora* 'Umbraculifera') in the background.

Contrasting forms add drama to a juxta-position of red daylily trumpets and the red-centered daisies of ox-eye sunflower (*Heliopsis helianthoides* 'Prairie Sunset').

ABOVE RIGHT

A dusting of pale blue calamint (*Nepeta calamintha* 'Blue Cloud') and the white flowers of tickseed (*Coreopsis* 'Snowberry') cool the warm colors of the Gold Border.

OPPOSITE

Touches of other, complementary colors are interwoven with the golds to furnish contrast and drama. Here *Coreopsis* 'Polaris' (front left) and *Coreopsis* 'Snowberry' (front right) supply a foreground for calamint (*Nepeta calamintha* 'Blue Cloud').

gardens and the Lurie Garden in Chicago's Millennium Park) has said that when he designs floral displays, he considers the forms of the flowers—their structures—before the colors. The design process at Wave Hill is, unlike Oudolf's carefully drafted plans, an organic one of setting out plants that have been judged to be compatible and mutually reinforcing and then arranging and sometimes rearranging them. But Wave Hill also favors structure. Bauer is quick to point out that the small, daisylike coreopsis, which blossoms in summer, is echoed by the daisylike flowers of the chrysanthemums in fall. There are the spikes of the camassias and eremurus, the floating globes of the allium flowers and the flattened parasols of the viburnums, the bowls of the crocuses and poppies. Attention to the flowers as sculptural elements enables a range of rhythms, harmonies, and contrasts complementary to those of the colors—a sort of visual counterpoint.

The Gold Border

It's also worth noting that the Gold Border, although the most prominent monochromatic display at Wave Hill, is not the only one. There is a small silver bed, a bed of plants with silvery gray foliage, on the west side of the glasshouses. For several years, the terrace to the west of Wave Hill House was also planted principally with silver-leaved Mediterranean and South African plants, although this display was brightened with the inclusion of gold-leaved plants as well. Set against a darker gray bluestone pavement, this display truly glowed.

What lessons for the home gardener are to be found in the Gold Border? Its changeability, the way in which it has evolved over the years with the ever-shifting balance between shrubs and perennials, is admirable. Bauer attributes this in large part to Wave Hill's evolutionary style of design. Because the Gold Border wasn't planted from a blueprint, it's not fixed. "It's always maturing, then needing renovation, then maturing again," he explains. "It's always somewhat in process."

An autumn view of the Hudson River and the Palisades from the top of the Gold Border, across the Kerlin Overlook.

ABOVE LEFT

Ox-eye sunflowers bloom at the foot of the umbrella Japanese red pine.

OPPOSITE

Another monochromatic composition is found in the silver bed to the west of the glasshouses. Here, Jerusalem sage (*Phlomis fruticosa*), background top, plays subtle harmonies with Andean silver-leaf sage (*Salvia discolor*), center left, dusty miller (*Senecio viravira*), center, licorice plant (*Helichrysum petiolare*), bottom left, and clasping heliotrope (*Heliotropium amplexicaule*), background bottom.

The Monocot and
Aquatic Gardens

PREVIOUS SPREAD

A venerable arborvitae (left) and a stately
elm (right) bracket the Monocot Garden,
serving as fixed points around which to
construct the display.

BELOW

Summertime in Wave Hill's Aquatic Garden.

F lowers routinely steal the limelight, but when all is said and done
it is usually the foliage that determines a plant's abiding presence.
If nothing else, the foliage tends to be present much more consistently.
This is true even with annual flowers but particularly so with perennials
and shrubs. Their bloom typically lasts just
weeks, while the foliage is present throughout
the growing season, or year-round in the
case of evergreens. Moreover, while foliage is
commonly regarded as a mere setting against
which to display flowers, in the hands of an
imaginative gardener, it can become the star.
This certainly is the case in Wave Hill's Aquatic
and Monocot Gardens.

These two displays, which share a space,
adjoin the north side of the Wild Garden, yet
are utterly different in character from that
feature. Whereas the Wild Garden contains its
naturalistic planting in an informal setting of
winding paths and irregular beds, the Aquatic
and Monocot Gardens inhabit a geometrically
regular oblong of roughly 9000 square feet
framed by stone and timber pergolas. Such
a formal setting may sound cold but the
effect is rather one of poise in the case of the
Aquatic Garden, while the geometrical beds
merely serve to emphasize the lushness of the
Monocot Garden's plantings.

A clipped hornbeam (*Carpinus betulus* 'Fastigiata') hedge backed by tall arborvitea closes the eastern end of the Aquatic Garden and screens it from the street.

ABOVE LEFT

Lotus (*Nelumbo nucifera*) leaves and seed pods stand sentry over the Aquatic Garden.

For that matter, just what is a monocot garden? Those with a knowledge of basic botany will recognize monocot as a term describing a plant whose embryo in the seed has just a single leaf. Monocots are one of the two major divisions of flowering plants; the other division, consisting of plants with two embryonic leaves, is called dicot. Other features common to monocots are flowers whose parts are borne in multiples of three, and, generally, a fibrous root system. Most notably, all monocots have leaves with parallel veins. (Dicots' veins are reticulate, forming nets.)

The more interesting question, of course, is not what, but why. Why plant a garden consisting solely of plants of this type? According to Marco Polo Stufano, that was the point when he and John Nally designed this feature: to make visitors aware of this botanical distinction. He and John had planted other educational gardens in this area. There had been, for example, a succotash garden, a combination of squash, beans, and corn interplanted according to a Native American model. Likewise, there had been a composite garden, a display composed entirely of plants with daisylike flowers. The Monocot Garden, however, achieved a greater impact. It fascinated visitors and even attracted funding from a local family, the Rossbachs, to enclose its two, flanking beds with stone paving punctuated with benches, and to make the Monocot Garden part of Wave Hill's permanent display.

Stufano attributes the appeal of this garden not primarily to its botanical definition, but rather to the monocots' special visual appeal. Monocots, he explains, have exceptionally beautiful, strong forms that play off each other. In designing an all-monocot display, he says, "you almost could do no wrong. Just throw them all together, although I hope we did more than that. They are very strong and wonderful pieces of sculpture to work with."

How could a garden visitor fail to find interest, for instance, in the so-called Swiss cheese plant, *Monstera deliciosa*, whose outsized leaves are as perforated with holes as the common name suggests? Or the spirally arranged leaves of the stepladder ginger (*Costus malortieanus*)? Or the Dr. Seuss–like tufts on sticks of the cabbage tree (*Cordyline australis*)? Such plants are indeed specimens of living sculpture.

Stufano describes the design process for this area as inspired by the plants themselves. "You start with the trees," or in this case, an arborvitae and an elm which are the most notable of the trees that back this feature, "and you work your way down. The way a picture is painted," he says. The image or the planting is built layer by layer. In the case of the garden, the space shaped by the trees is punctuated by the taller plants, such as cannas (*Canna* 'Le Roi Humbert', for instance) and coconut palm (*Cocos nucifera*). A layer of midsized plants is then disposed: bananas (*Musa* 'Truly Tiny' and 'Siam Beauty') and variegated corn (*Zea mays* 'Japanese Variegated'), for example. Finally, shorter plants, such as Mexican speckled wandering Jew (*Tinantia pringlei*), daylilies (*Hemerocallis* 'Autumn King'), and blackberry lily (*Iris domestica*) are arranged around the feet of the taller plants.

The main challenge in the Monocot Garden is keeping the foliage interesting—placing the right plants side by side to create harmonies,

OPPOSITE

The southern end of the Monocot Garden, a display defined by its botany.

BELOW

The Rossbach Monocot Garden.

BOTTOM

Two beds of monocots flank a stone-paved seating area.

The monocots' strong leaf forms turn this garden into a sculptural display.

contrasts, and rhythms, and managing the variety of heights. This creates a kind of sculptural display, more than in some of the other gardens. Curly, thin leaves are next to straight-up swords, which are next to ruffled, wide leaves. Foliage colors, such as silver and green and gold, come into play, too.

Jen Cimino, the gardener who cares for the Monocot Garden—and the Aquatic Garden, too—declares that

The Monocot and Aquatic Gardens

Two displays share a space: from the southeast, the Aquatic Garden in front, the Monocot Garden and surrounding pergolas beyond.

she likes playing off textures, the effect of the foliage in aggregate. It's surely no coincidence that she has had a longstanding interest in black-and-white photography, in which form and light and texture play central roles.

There is, for example, the contrast of the fine, ribbonlike grasses such as big bluestem (*Andropogon gerardii*), eyelash grass (*Bouteloua gracilis*), feather reed grass (*Calamagrostis ×acutiflora* 'Karl Foerster'), Idaho fescue (*Festuca idahoensis*), and *Festuca glauca*, with the broad, ruffled leaves of the alocasias—*Alocasia macrorrhiza* 'Lutea', *A.* 'Portodora', and *A. wentii* (Went's hardy elephant ear). There are subtler contrasts, too, such as those of form within the single texture of the blade-shaped foliages: the squat sunburst of the yucca (*Yucca filamentosa*) versus the six-foot tufts of New Zealand flax (*Phormium tenax* 'Radiance') and the tall stalks of the song of India plant (*Dracaena reflexa*).

There are contrasts of foliage colors as well: all shades of green and variegated leaves, such as the yellow-striped blades of Chilean iris (*Libertia ixioides* 'Goldfinger') and the white-striped ones of basket grass (*Oplismenus hirtellus* 'Variegatus'); bold reds, as in the red-stalked

The Monocot and Aquatic Gardens

LEFT TO RIGHT

Strong contrasts characterize this group of monocots; here, a Eurasian import, black false hellebore (*Veratrum nigrum*), raises its purple-black flower stems.

Trumpet lily (*Lilium longiflorum*) blossoms silhouetted against leaves of hardy banana (*Musa basjoo*). Creating foliar and floral harmonies, contrasts, and rhythms is a key to the Monocot Garden.

Monocot floral parts are borne in multiples of three. Seen here, the six-petaled blossoms of the blackberry lily (*Iris domestica*).

Scarlet blossoms of *Crocosmia* 'Lucifer' bloom and rebloom throughout the summer.

Sometimes called Turk's cap lilies because of the turbanlike form of the blossoms, martagon lilies (*Lilium martagon*) bloom in the Monocot Garden in early summer to midsummer.

elephant ear (*Colocasia esculenta* 'Red Rhubarb') and the leaves of red banana (*Ensete ventricosum* 'Maurelii'); and the purples of the bromeliad *Alcantarea* 'Malbec' and purple-leaved sugar cane (*Saccharum officinarum* 'Pele's Smoke'). There is even near-black to be found, such as in the mondo grass *Ophiopogon planiscapus* 'Ebony Knight'.

All of this is not to say that flowers have no role in the Monocot Garden. They do, but more as a spice than a staple. Louis Bauer cites the "fireworks" of the *Lilium henryi* var. *citrinum* blossoms when that wild-type lily is in full bloom. The backswept petals, lemon-yellow and brown-flecked, borne in luxurious clusters on eight-foot stems at midsummer, are spectacular though short-lived. More persistent are the violet-blue clusters of the blue ginger (*Dichorisandra thyrsiflora*), which keep opening through the hot weather. Or the gladiolus-like, scarlet blossoms of *Crocosmia* 'Lucifer' and the burnt-orange flowers of *C.* 'Emberglow', which bloom and re-bloom throughout the summer. For a day-in, day-out show, however, it is the foliage that carries the weight.

Another notable aspect of this garden is the contribution made by tropical plants. Cimino is also the curator of the Tropical House in Wave Hill's

conservatory, and many of the plants that overwinter there spend their summers in the Monocot Garden. Indeed, more than half of the plants that make a regular appearance in this display come from the Tropical House, and just as the summer visitors change from year to year, so does the Monocot Garden.

Curiously, although potted plants also play an important role in the adjacent Aquatic Garden, in the latter space they are more commonly drawn from the conservatory's Succulent House. The reason for this, surely, is the Aquatic Garden's more architectural setting. The pool, which measures 40 feet by 25 feet, is, like the pergolas to its north and south, a survivor from Wave Hill's days as a private estate. When Marco Polo Stufano first encountered it, it was surrounded by a bed filled with variegated iris. He dug these out and tried to replace them with more interesting plantings, initially a collection of scented geraniums. Visitors, though, could not resist walking through the bed to reach the edge of the pool and inspect its resident fish and frogs. Eventually, the planting was replaced with bluestone paving, which was later extended into a terrace on the pool's eastern end, bounded by a clipped hedge of European hornbeam (*Carpinus betulus* 'Fastigiata').

OPPOSITE

Succulents in containers serve as garden statuary, staged around and in the Aquatic Garden.

BELOW

The Aquatic Garden at midsummer, from the west. Surrounding plantings were replaced with bluestone paving so that visitors could approach to view frogs, tadpoles, and fish.

Such a built environment, with its carefully ruled lines and broad, flat surfaces of water and pavement, is perfect for the display of sculptural plants like those found in the Succulent House. It's a pedestal writ large. Moreover, the stone pavement can also be hot and arid in midsummer, conditions to which the succulents are better adapted than other plants. And, the contrast between the aquatic plants in the pool and the dryland plants around it is powerfully dramatic.

Drama is continued in the pool itself. The water is black; Cimino darkens it with a powdered black mineral to inhibit algae growth and also to screen the fish and frogs from the gaze of herons

Gardening with Tropicals

Nighttime temperatures, says Wave Hill gardener Jen Cimino, are crucial to determining when she moves tropical plants into the Monocot Garden in the springtime. The temperatures should remain above 50°F. When the weather has warmed to this point, Jen first moves the potted tropicals to a cooler glasshouse than the one in which they have spent the winter. (A semi-heated sunroom would serve for a home gardener.) After a couple of weeks there, the pots are moved again, this time outdoors into the filtered light under an expanse of shade cloth. This second step allows the tropical plants to acclimate to the stronger light they will encounter in the outdoor environment. A patch of filtered light underneath a high tree canopy would serve as well. Moving the plants directly into full sun would cause the foliage to sunburn, and look unattractive until it could regrow, perhaps not until late summer.

Once the plants are acclimated, usually in May or June, they are moved to the garden. Jen slips them from their pots, taking the opportunity to divide any that have bulked up over the winter indoors. Then the tropicals are planted in selected areas of the beds. Careful irrigation is critical at this point; the root systems of the newly transplanted tropicals are limited and the cool conditions reduce the plants' need for water. Overwatering could be fatal. Fertilizing is also begun at this time: a dilute solution of a water-soluble, complete plant food is applied every two weeks.

Irrigation becomes more frequent, as much as daily, by midsummer. As the weather cools, and overnight temperatures drop again to around 50°F, Cimino digs the tropicals from the beds, divides those that have increased over the summer, and repots them. Then it's back to the glasshouse for winter storage—except for the red banana, which has its leaves removed and is left dormant in a pile of leaves in a frost-free garage.

Native as far north as Nova Scotia, pickerel weed (*Pontederia cordata*) overwinters in the pool, to be lifted and separated in spring.

ABOVE LEFT

Floating on the black surface, the flamboyant foliage and flower of this tropical water lily (*Nymphaea* 'Foxfire') resemble one of Mary Delany's "paper mosaiks."

and other predators. But the flat, black surface also provides a perfect canvas on which to display the foliage of the aquatic plants: the broad, notched disks of the water lilies (*Nymphaea* cultivars), the heart-shaped leaves of the aptly named yellow floating heart (*Nymphoides peltata*), and the intricate patterns of the mosaic plant (*Ludwigia sedioides*). Hovering above these are the large, parasol-like leaves of the sacred lotus (*Nelumbo nucifera*) and the American lotus (*Nelumbo lutea*), the fine-textured puffs of papyrus (*Cyperus papyrus*), the darts of the broadleaf arrowhead (*Sagittaria latifolia*), the white- and green-striped uprights of the variegated sweet flag (*Acorus calamus* 'Variegatus'), and the skinny straps of the narrowleaf cattail (*Typha angustifolia*).

Bauer likens the effect of the leaves on the black background to the work of the 18th-century botanical illustrator Mrs. Mary Delany. Delany, an associate of Sir Joseph Banks, the greatest British botanist of his day,

created what she called "paper mosaiks" by cutting out and gluing bits of colored paper to a black background; the results were plant images of startling verisimilitude and great elegance. There is a similar, deliberately theatrical quality to Wave Hill's Aquatic Garden, especially since a number of exotic species have been included in its planting.

Staged so that its pot seems to rest on the surface of the water, for example, is a spidery blue sotol (*Dasylirion berlandieri*). Set just into the water are pots of insectivorous pitcher plants: two cultivars of the yellow pitcher plant (*Sarracenia flava* var. *flava* and *Sarracenia flava* var. *ornata* 'LW5'), as well as a cut-throat yellow pitcher plant (*Sarracenia flava* var. *rugelii*). Floating on the water's surface are plumes of parrot feather (*Myriophyllum* species), finely cut fronds of aquatic sensitive plant (*Neptunia aquatica*) and crisp heads of water lettuce (*Pistia stratiotes*). Standing erect nearby are variegated umbrella plant (*Cyperus alternifolius* 'Variegatus'), elephant ears (*Colocasia* species), and cannas (*Canna* species) that Cimino's predecessor grew from seed collected onsite, as well as two kinds of papyrus (*Cyperus* species). With such neighbors, the vivid colors of the water lilies—reds, yellows, fuchsia, and white—and the creamy yellow bowls of the sacred lotus, eight inches or more in diameter, seem not over-the-top but perfectly in tune.

The serene scene has a timeless quality, especially when visited on a still day when dragonflies hover over the water, but Stufano marvels at how this garden has changed over the years. Most of the plants are now grown in containers; the larger aquatics, such as the water lilies, are planted in plastic crates lined with landscape fabric and filled with loam. This means that gardener Cimino can rearrange them to her taste each spring, in part to suit whatever tropicals and succulents she has brought out from the conservatory to summer here. Similarly, she annually changes many of the tropical plants that she places in the Monocot Garden, giving it a fresh aspect every year.

Beyond the carefully clipped hornbeam hedge that marks the Aquatic Garden's eastern boundary is a whimsical footnote, furnished by an even more creative use of containers. Here, at the back entrance to the Monocot and Aquatic Gardens, Jen Cimino has assembled a row of free-form tripods she fashioned from grapevine trunks, prunings from the trellis that surrounds this area. Interspersed with these are containers she made from hollow logs and stumps, into which she chiseled recesses. The

OPPOSITE

The Aquatic Garden, from the east. The flat, black surface of the water provides a giant pedestal for the display of foliages and container plants.

Staged just above the surface of the pool, blue sotol (*Dasylirion berlandieri*) inscribes a neat fountain of foliage between a cluster of lotus leaves (left) and *Oryza sativa* 'Red Dragon' (right); this pitcher plant (*Sarracenia flava* 'Cut Throat') seems to stand balanced on its own reflection; gardener Jen Cimino grew these cannas from seed collected onsite; eight-inch blossoms of lotus (*Nelumbo* 'Green Maiden') seem right at home; lotus leaf disks juxtapose with the variegated blades of sweet flag (*Acorus calamus* 'Variegatus').

crannies were then fitted with bromeliads, tropical plants that naturally grow without soil, inhabiting crevices in trees and rocks. The grapevine tripods she used as trellises to support scarlet-flowered, climbing cypress vine (*Ipomoea quamoclit*). These elements provide another, last play on textures—the foliage of the cypress vine is fine and feathery, that of the bromeliads thick, almost fleshy, and borne typically in rosettes. A spot

Caring for Aquatics

In March or April, the hardy plants that have overwintered in the Aquatic Garden pool are lifted from its depths. Roots are taken out of their plastic milk crates full of soil. Some root systems, such as those of the sacred lotus (*Nelumbo nucifera*), can be pulled apart and divided by hand. Others, such as the pickerel weed (*Pontederia cordata*) and the robust root system that usually fills its crate, require a sharp spade for cutting into pieces.

After their roots are divided, aquatic plants are repotted in crates lined with landscape fabric and filled with topsoil. A cupful of dehydrated cow manure is mixed into each soil-filled crate, the roots are buried, and the contents are top-dressed with a half-inch of fine gravel so that the soil underneath does not cloud the water. Finally, a slow-release fertilizer tablet specially formulated for aquatics is slipped into the soil in each crate. Monthly thereafter, the dose is repeated, until September.

The plants that are too tender to winter in the pool fall into two groups. The first group consists of true aquatics, such as the tropical water lilies. These are also cultivated in crates, but require overwintering conditions for which Wave Hill has no facilities, so they are simply replaced with new stock every spring. The second group is comprised of plants that are adapted to grow in water—or at the water margins, such as papyrus (*Cyperus papyrus*). These are cultivated in pots. The potted plants are removed as the pool water chills in October, and pots are relocated to the frost-free sunroom attached to the south side of Glyndor House, one of the former residences on the Wave Hill estate, now used for gallery and office space. If plants are pot-bound, they are divided and repotted, in the same fashion as the hardy plants. Afterward, pots are placed in saucers full of water to keep them moist. In late April or early May, when the air warms, the pots go back into the pool, and the cycle begins again.

The use of containers also allows the removal and indoor overwintering of some of the less-than-hardy plants. The sotol, for instance, goes back to the Succulent House. Others, such as the parrot feather and water lettuce, are just replaced annually.

BELOW, LEFT TO RIGHT

More than just an architectural frame, the pergolas surrounding these gardens are an opportunity for planting. Here they support a fall flock of gourds.

The pergola provides a home for many vines, including *Campsis radicans* 'Crimson Trumpet'.

This pergola is a shady retreat in hot weather and frames the composition of bromeliads at the far end.

The Monocot and Aquatic Gardens

The strictly geometrical surround emphasizes the romantic lushness of the pool in the Aquatic Garden, even here, before the hedge has received its midsummer trim.

was also found here for a drape of Spanish moss (*Tillandsia usneoides*), which despite its appearance is not a moss but rather a bromeliad as well.

Nowhere at Wave Hill is the tension between formality and informality used more effectively. The Wild Garden next door, with its informal layout and planting, might seem the obvious means for visitors to reinsert themselves into the natural world, and it is. But the pool, with the fish and tadpoles emerging momentarily at the surface of the black water and then disappearing back into the depths, has its own transformative magic. Likewise, the clean surfaces and crisp lines of the surroundings make this a perfect backdrop for the theatricality of a sacred lotus or a pitcher plant; the contrast only emphasizes the jungle exoticism of the tropicals in the monocot beds. When Stufano and Nally designed this area, according to Louis Bauer, they were reaching for something that people hadn't seen before. Certainly they, and gardeners like Jen Cimino who have followed them, have achieved that.

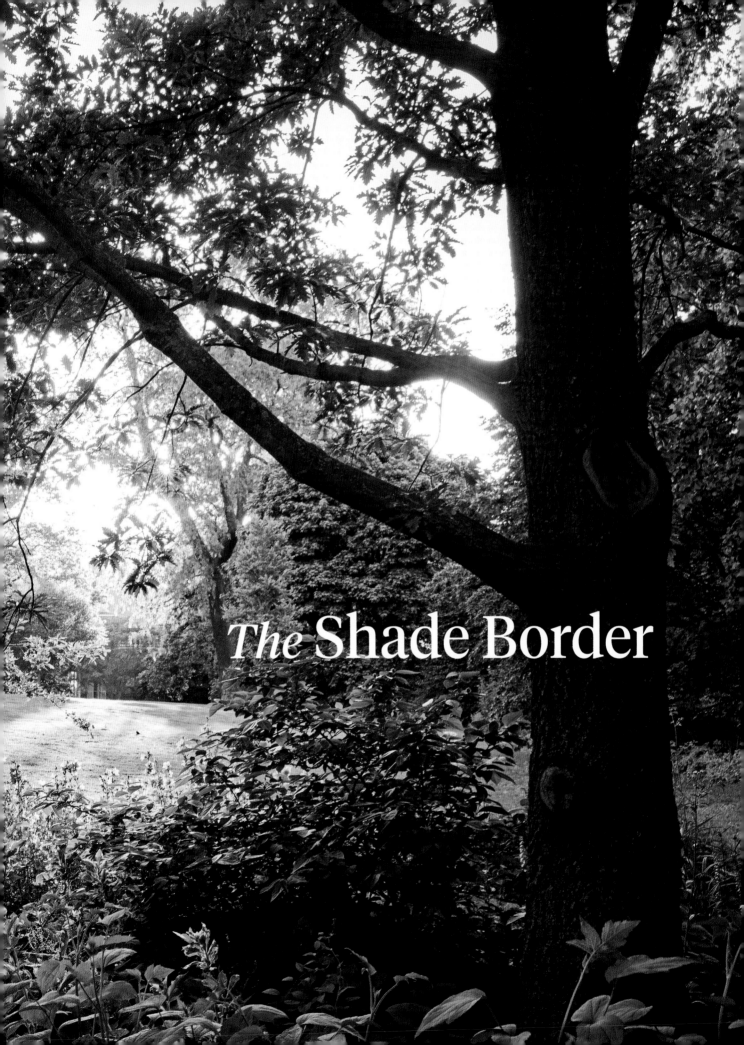

The Shade Border

PREVIOUS SPREAD

Beautiful in all four seasons, Wave Hill's
Shade Border demonstrates the potential
for gardening in lower light.

OPPOSITE

Spanish bluebells (*Hyacinthoides
hispanica*) bloom in early May along the
south end of the Shade Border's north-
south path.

The gardeners at Wave Hill knew better. Visitors kept excusing their own lack of a garden by pleading that their yards offered no sun, only shade, yet the staff gardeners knew a shaded planting could be as rich as any other. And so, a couple of years before Marco Polo Stufano retired in 2001, he and his staff began planting interesting and attractive shade-tolerant plants in an area under the trees at the perimeter of the old estate grounds, just to the north and east of Wave Hill House, the original residence. Thus was born what would become the Shade Border.

There was ample opportunity. Wave Hill is notable for its magnificent trees, and a series of venerable elms (*Ulmus americana*) shaded most of the area in question. Ultimately, all of these except one fell victim to Dutch elm disease, but a program of planting replaced those trees with deciduous and evergreen fellows, largely deep-rooted oaks that invited underplanting. Shade-tolerant shrubs from an area of the grounds under redevelopment were moved to serve as an understory, and two long borders were staked out, edging an L-shaped path some 300 feet long. The longer leg ran east and west and a shorter leg ran due south. At the 90-degree elbow, Louis Bauer designed a curved arbor to provide delightful, shady seating and to anchor this corner of the property.

Shade gardens and their plantings are defined by the degree of light they receive. Sunlight is the fuel that powers the growth of nearly all plants, just as gasoline drives the typical car, and as with gasoline, sunlight comes in a number of different octanes. In general, gardeners distinguish just three grades. There is high octane, what gardeners call full sun, found in areas that receive direct, unfiltered sunlight through at least six hours of every day. Then there is the less intense partial shade, more or less synonymous with the term "partial sun." Partial-shade areas

The Shade Border

The west-to-east leg of the Shade Border's L-shaped path.

The red leaves of Japanese spice-bush (*Lindera obtusiloba*) enhance photosynthesis.

Flame azalea (*Rhododendron calendulaceum*) flourishes in an area of dappled shade.

receive three to six hours of direct sunlight per day. Full-shade areas receive less than three hours of direct sunlight daily.

According to Bauer, however, such a simple hierarchy is far too crude. It does not take into account, for instance, the time of day when the area receives sunlight; the sun is more intense in the afternoon than in the morning. An area that receives its sunlight from noon to six in the evening, for instance, is much more high-test than one that receives its sunlight from six in the morning to noon. Apart from timing, too, shade varies in quality with what casts it. Shade cast by a building or wall, or even by evergreens, remains fairly uniform throughout the day, whereas shade cast by deciduous trees, especially if the canopy of branches

The Shade Border

is high and thin, tends to vary over the course of a day, letting a lot of filtered or dappled light penetrate to any plant located underneath.

Deciduous shade also varies with the seasons, of course. A spot under the canopy of an oak tree may be shady in the summertime when the tree is in leaf, but during the period from late fall through mid- to late spring when the oak leaves are absent, it receives full sun just slightly filtered by the shadows of the branches. This is important, because there is a wealth of understory plants that have adapted to that seasonal schedule, plants that make their growth during the period when the trees overhead are leafless. These include winter annuals: plants that germinate in the fall, make growth during the relatively warmer periods of the winter, and bloom and set seed in early spring. More important from the gardener's perspective are the so-called spring ephemerals. This is a class of perennial plants that emerge from dormancy early in the spring, grow rapidly, only to flower and then return to dormancy in late spring.

OPPOSITE

Another shade-adapted shrub, dwarf fothergilla (*Fothergilla gardenii*) bears white and greenish flowers.

BELOW

Many of the woody plants that thrive in shade, such as this oakleaf hydrangea (*Hydrangea quercifolia*), bear white, creamy, slightly greenish blossoms.

The length of the leafless season of different types of trees, and the plants it will support, also varies. Some trees remain leafless longer into spring than others. As a rule, the trees native to Wave Hill leaf out later than many of the exotic species; exotics often have come from warmer, more southerly regions where spring comes sooner. At least one species, the overcup oak (*Quercus lyrata*) is the exception that proves the rule. This tree, naturally indigenous from New Jersey southward, leafs out later in the spring than its fellows. Coming across it in springtime, those inexperienced with it might think it has died. The overcup that was planted in the area of the Shade Border almost two decades ago now provides an exceptionally long window of sunlight beneath its branches.

DRY VERSUS MOIST SHADE

By sheltering the ground from dehydrating sunlight, shade can contribute to moist conditions in the soil. Likewise, the leaf litter that accumulates under many trees acts as a mulch to help prevent the soil from drying out. Many of the most interesting types of shade plants flourish in moist shade. Variegated Japanese butterbur (*Petasites japonicus* 'Variegatus'), for example, requires a consistently moist soil: it bears six-inch-tall stalks of yellowish white, daisylike flowers in April, before its yellow-splashed, 18-inch, shieldlike leaves emerge. So does its North American equivalent, the so-called umbrella plant (*Darmera peltata*), which also flowers before the leaves emerge, following its steroidal lollipops of pink to white flowers with three- to five-foot mounds of 18-inch, umbrella-like leaves. These also require partial to full shade.

Trees whose roots run close to the surface of the soil, however, such as maples and beeches, can work like pumps to suck the moisture out of the soil, leading to the condition known as dry shade. Slightly less difficult are the conditions found under deeper-rooted oaks and hornbeams. Evergreens like spruce and hemlock also may have shallow roots; moreover, their dense, year-round canopies can act like umbrellas to keep precipitation from falling on the soil beneath them. Dry shade, especially that cast by evergreens, is a challenging habitat for most plants, and the species that flourish in it are relatively few. Susannah Strazzera, the gardener at Wave Hill who currently has charge of the Shade Border, has found that applying a thick mulch of semi-decomposed leaves—ideally oak—can help keep the surface soil in dry shade areas moister, enhancing growth in such locations. To supply this mulch, Wave Hill stacks all the leaves the gardeners rake up in fall, letting them age before use. Wave Hill also accepts leaves from

Variegated Japanese butterbur (*Petasites japonicus* 'Variegatus', right center) makes a bold statement in moist shade, bearing yellowish white flowers in April before its large, yellow-splashed leaves emerge.

OPPOSITE

Primula bulleyana is another ornament of moist shade.

neighborhood landscapers; usually these have been shredded by the vacuums the landscapers use to collect them and they make a particularly good mulch.

SPRING BLOOMERS

A mainstay of shady gardens is the collection of plants that take advantage of the seasonal sunshine under deciduous trees, making most of their growth during late winter through midspring. This category includes many early spring–flowering bulbs, such as crocuses and snowdrops (*Galanthus* species). Because these are such a feature of Wave Hill's Wild Garden (see the following chapter), and because Wave Hill prefers to adopt a different plant palette for each garden, they have not been used in the Shade Border. Instead, the Shade Border revels in the early spring wildflowers common in northern woodlands.

Some of these are natives of northeastern North America, such as trilliums (*Trillium* species) and wild ginger (*Asarum canadense*). This is not a native-plants display, however, and many of the wildflowers blooming here in early spring are natives of the Old World, particularly eastern Asia. This bespeaks a bit of geologic history. At one time (175–335 million years ago), most of the landmasses which now make up the continents of the northern hemisphere were united in one supercontinent, Laurasia, and shared a common flora. Remnants of this common flora persist today in eastern Asia and our own eastern North American deciduous forest.

The connection remains close: DNA studies have found, for example, that over half of the trees and shrubs native to the southern Appalachians trace their ancestry to Asian plants. Maples (*Acer* species), rhododendrons (*Rhododendron* species), viburnums (*Viburnum* species), and magnolias (*Magnolia* species) are just a few examples of common garden plants with representatives in both regions. Perhaps because its topography and climate are more diverse, though, eastern Asia has spawned a far more diverse flora—there are more than twice as many species of flowering plants native to that region than in eastern North America. That makes Asian flora a treasure house of adapted plants for American gardeners, plants that integrate easily into our northeastern landscape and vegetation. Strazzera and her predecessors have taken full advantage of that fact.

OPPOSITE, CLOCKWISE FROM TOP LEFT

Dry-shade performers: spring-blooming Siberian bugloss (*Brunnera macrophylla*); Japanese painted fern (*Athyrium nipponicum* var. *pictum*) prefers moisture in spring but tolerates dry shade in summer; 'Rose Queen' bishop's hat (*Epimedium grandiflorum*); hostas tolerate dry summers in shade.

BELOW

Bottlebrush buckeye (*Aesculus parviflora*), one of the few shrubs that thrives in dry shade.

In this, they have run counter to the current fashion of planting only native North American plants in North American gardens. This is not to say that Wave Hill has ignored that trend. It has created a natives-only area (with a twist) in the Elliptical Garden, and plans have been made to eventually install more native plants in Wave Hill's woodland areas, as budget and personnel permit. But the Shade Border has always been, and remains, frankly cosmopolitan.

This has advantages. For one thing, it has allowed for an extension of the flowering season. Native North American plants such as wild ginger (*Asarum canadense*), trout lilies (*Erythronium americanum*), Virginia bluebells (*Mertensia virginica*), and flame azaleas (*Rhododendron calendulaceum*) contribute heavily to the early spring to midspring show, but Asian natives such as bleeding hearts (*Lamprocapnos spectabilis*), yellow wax bells (*Kirengeshoma palmata*), and enkianthus (*Enkianthus* species) make up a disproportionate part of the summer display. Because the Asian and eastern American floras overlap, the various plants intermingle comfortably. Asian relatives of our native Jack-in-the-pulpit (*Arisaema triphyllum*), such as the Japanese cobra lily (*Arisaema ringens*), although larger and more flamboyant, still

OPPOSITE

The Shade Border is flush with early spring flowers, among them great white trillium (*Trillium grandiflorum*) and dwarf fothergilla (front) backed by a sea of forget-me-nots (*Myosotis scorpioides*).

BELOW, LEFT TO RIGHT

A trio of trilliums in spring (from left): red trillium (*Trillium erectum*) follows its bloom with a dark maroon, berrylike fruit; great white trillium (*Trillium grandiflorum*) thrives in moist but well-drained, organic-rich soil; the main attraction of *Trillium sessile* is its whorl of marbled leaves.

OPPOSITE, CLOCKWISE FROM TOP LEFT

A native woodland ground cover, dwarf crested iris (*Iris cristata*) supplies a blue note to the Shade Border in early spring.

Spanish bluebells (*Hyacinthoides hispanica*) are, as the name indicates, natives of the Iberian Peninsula, growing best in well-drained soils in sun-dappled, partial shade.

Originating in Siberia, northern China, and Japan, bleeding heart adds a cosmopolitan touch to the Shade Border in spring. The whole form (*Lamprocapnos spectabilis* 'Alba') is pictured here.

Fairy bells (*Disporum flavens*) from Korea dangle their yellow blossoms over the lavender-blue of woodland phlox (*Phlox divaricata*) in this early-spring combination.

ABOVE LEFT

Outstanding as a woodland ground cover, *Geranium maculatum* combines deeply cut, palmately lobed, dark-green leaves with midspring, one-and-a-quarter-inch, five-petaled lilac to pink flowers. Native to northeastern North America.

ABOVE

Flame azalea (*Rhododendron calendulaceum*) in full, midspring bloom.

Thriving in part to full shade, yellow wax bells (*Kirengeshoma palmata*) make a tall (to four feet) shrubby perennial that blooms in summer or early fall. Native to Korea and Japan.

ABOVE RIGHT

Native to Chinese woodlands, upright wild ginger (*Saruma henryi*) bears its yellow flowers in early spring to midspring, and will often repeat bloom in late summer. The rounded, heart-shaped leaves are equally decorative.

OPPOSITE

Often called cobra lilies because of the likeness of their flowers to a snake's hooded head, Asian arisaemas flourish in the Shade Border's partial-shade areas.

look very much at home in this deciduous woodland setting. Similarly, as the season progresses, native mayapples (*Podophyllum peltatum*) give way seamlessly to Himalayan and Chinese variants (*Podophyllum hexandrum* and *P. pleianthum*).

Backing up the flowering is a wonderful variety of foliages. Long after their flowers have finished, four species of North American trilliums carpet the ground with their neat, triplet leaves, intermingling with Chinese wild gingers (*Saruma henryi*), whose heart-shaped leaves are silver when they emerge in spring, only gradually settling into green. *Sauromatum venosum*, the so-called voodoo lily of India, does flower, sending up a three-foot stalk in early June that unfurls to reveal a purplish black, spiked spadix cloaked by a marbled, yellow and purple hood; but after the bloom fades, it is the large, tropical-looking,

OPPOSITE, CLOCKWISE FROM TOP LEFT

This sweet gum cultivar (*Liquidambar styraciflua* 'Gum Ball') with a dense, compact, bushy head of branches, is outstanding for its late fall foliage color.

Marking the beginning of autumn, the "flowers" (actually, sterile sepals) of the oakleaf hydrangea (*Hydrangea quercifolia*) blush pink.

Native witch hazel (*Hamamelis virginiana*) blooms in late fall.

The berries of this cotoneaster (*Cotoneaster salicifolius* var. *rugosus*) are vivid attractions of the Shade Border in fall.

fingered leaves (borne on purple-speckled stems) that earns this plant a spot through the rest of the growing season.

AUTUMN COLOR

The floral display of the Shade Border is limited in fall, although the plumbago (*Ceratostigma plumbaginoides*) continues to produce blue flowers into October, when it is joined by the ageratum-like blue mist-flower (*Conoclinium coelestinum*), blue-flowered *Geranium* 'Gerwat' ROZANNE, the red-veined pink blossoms of *Geranium* 'Tiny Monster', and the red-and-yellow-flowered Indian pink (*Spigelia marilandica*). Foliage color more than makes up for any flagging bloom. There are the bronzy reds of the oakleaf hydrangeas (*Hydrangea quercifolia*), the scarlet and purple of the sweet gum trees (*Liquidambar styraciflua*), the deep red of the plumbago foliage in November, and the pinks, reds, and magentas of the yellow root (*Xanthorhiza simplicissima*). *Amsonia* 'Blue Ice', whose flowers contributed constellations of dark lavender-blue flowers in June, now adds a clear note of yellow as its foliage turns before dormancy.

COLOR FROM FRUITS

A subtler but still significant factor of this garden's display is its colorful fruits. The sources of these are many. Shadbush (*Amelanchier canadensis*), in addition to supplying clusters of white, five-petaled flowers in April, subsequently produces fruits that ripen from green to red and finally to purplish black in early summer. The fruits of the spicebush (*Lindera benzoin*) are red now, as are the fruits of the *Trillium* species, including *Trillium cuneatum*, *T. sessile*, *T. erectum*, and *T. grandiflorum*. Spikes of scarlet berries are also contributed by the cobra lilies (*Arisaema* species).

Other colorful fruits include the red-stemmed, white fruits of the baneberry (*Actaea pachypoda*) that follow its terminal clusters of white flowers in mid- to late spring, and the red, berrylike fruits of the viburnums (*Viburnum* 'Cayuga', *V. dilatatum*, *V. lantana*, and *V. ×rhytidophylloides*). Strazzera's favorite among the shrubs are the yellow-orange berries of a winterberry (*Ilex verticillata* 'Winter Gold'). This last, incidentally, holds its fruit well into the winter, providing yet another season of color.

PLANTING AND CARE

Gardening is different in the shade. The fundamental rules still apply: matching the right plant to the right location and building a community of compatible species. But in the shade, special dynamics also come into play. Soil preparation in the shade garden, for example, is as much a case of building up as digging down.

Of course, digging is difficult in most shady areas because the soils are infiltrated with tree roots. These can be severed with a sharpened spade or with a pair of lopping shears, but to do so injures the overhanging tree, so this should not be done more than is necessary. The Wave Hill gardeners have found two ways to reduce the need for digging. One is to build up the soil by working copious amounts of compost and dehydrated cow manure into its surface—this creates a plantable layer without disturbing the tree roots below. The other strategy is to plant small. Strazzera likes to dig the soil to twice the depth of the root ball of any plant she is installing. If she plants "plugs," small seedlings grown in cells in a plastic tray, then she doesn't have to disturb the soil nearly as deeply as she does with older plants grown in larger nursery containers.

It's important to know your soil. The soil in the Shade Border is tested annually and, because soils can vary from spot to spot, when the soil is tested, samples are taken from several places. This allows the gardeners to identify, for example, areas where the soil is more acidic in pH, so that they can target such areas for planting with acid-loving plants such as rhododendrons, hollies, and enkianthus. Deciduous and evergreen, these shrubs help structure the Shade Border.

The fertilization program is flexible. Typically, a granular organic fertilizer is spread in spring, and sometimes also in the fall if the growth of a particular plant seems less than robust. Conversely, when a plant is growing especially well, fertilization may be skipped altogether.

Irrigation, however, is indispensable. There is no irrigation system in the Shade Border; to install one would require cutting countless tree roots. As a result, all the watering is done with hoses, portable sprinklers, and sometimes soaker hoses in the case of new plantings. During dry spells, a special point is made of watering beneath all the trees because not only do they otherwise suffer, they will also draw all the moisture from the ground beneath them, parching the ground-floor plants below.

The view east through the autumnal Shade Border.

Here, oak leaves are used whole around evergreen Himalayan maidenhair fern (*Adiantum venustum*) under shrubs. Unshredded leaf mulches may be used in shrubbery areas because of their greater durability.

As has already been mentioned, chopped-leaf mulch plays an essential role in this garden, and not only in the areas of dry shade. Applied throughout the Shade Border, it not only helps to conserve moisture, but, as it decomposes, it adds a layer of humus to the soil surface in which the smaller woodland plants flourish. This mulch is especially important around the plants that prefer moist shade. Timing is important in the spreading of this material: it is done in very early spring so that the smaller spring wildflowers are not disturbed or buried.

The final, and most persistent task faced in this border is weeding. This is particularly important along the southern edge of the border, where it adjoins the lawn, because the extra sun received there fuels stronger weed growth. Even within the border's shaded interior, however,

The Shade Border

careful editing is essential to keep the more aggressive spreaders, such as Siberian bugloss, from overrunning their neighbors, while leaving a ground cover dense enough to resist invasives. Indeed, Strazzera explicitly warns against accepting gift plants billed as "so easy to grow" until you have thoroughly researched them and made sure they are not thugs.

The character of this border is always changing. As trees mature and age, the character of their canopies changes, growing denser, perhaps, or thinner. Some of the deciduous trees, such as the elms, have died, opening gaps in the canopy that are only partially plugged by the planting of new specimens. Evergreens such as arborvitaes (*Thuja occidentalis*), planted decades ago to screen the view of the street that runs along the north and east borders, have outgrown their spots and are gradually being removed, lightening the shade locally and creating new areas for planting.

Dealing with this change is partly a deliberate program of adding or moving plants. To a large extent, though, the plants relocate themselves, seeding themselves into spots where the degree of light suits them better and disappearing from others that have become unsuitable because of changes in the canopy.

In short, the plants know best what they want. The gardener can guess at the best match between the degree and kind of shade in a location and the species that will flourish there, but ultimately, the plants find their own niches.

Even in winter, the Shade Border is not completely without bloom: *Camellia* 'Survivor'.

OPPOSITE

OPPOSITE

A scattering of oak leaves carpets the arbor in the Shade Border, before being gathered as mulch.

ABOVE

Shade Border gardener Susannah Strazzera's cold weather favorite: winterberry (*Ilex verticillata* 'Winter Gold').

The Wild Garden

PREVIOUS SPREAD

Cascading down a slope, the Wild Garden
offers a round-the-world trip in a little more
than a dozen rich beds.

OPPOSITE

The Wild Garden's panoramic view is
carefully rationed, revealed at strategic
points in the twisting paths, and only fully
shared at the gazebo at the garden's crest.

E ven for Wave Hill, the site is dramatic: a cascade of more than
a dozen beds spilling down a southwest-facing hillside with a
panoramic view of the Hudson River. And make no mistake, this garden
is fully as extraordinary as the setting.

Visitors expect that when entering Wave Hill's Wild Garden they will see
a meadow mix of plants that are a little unkempt. But what they experience is a journey halfway round the world, with all sorts of plant niches
represented. Every few steps, they're in a different habitat, a different
combination of plants.

It's a unique experience because this horticultural travelogue is not laid
out in a predictable row or grid. Instead, the beds are irregular, the narrow paths that divide them meandering, crisscrossing, and full of twists
and turns. "It's intricate," says Louis Bauer of the design, "and unfolds a
little at a time." As a result, to walk the paths here is to make a series of
small but delightful discoveries, the experience changing bed by bed.

In many respects this is a beginning point—the Wild Garden was the
first planting project that Marco Polo Stufano and John Nally undertook
after renovating the glasshouses and creating the conservatory. In point
of fact, the bones of the garden predate even that. Not long after adding
the acreage that completed the estate as it now stands, owner George
Perkins hired Albert Millard, a Viennese-born landscape gardener, to
help him bring order to the patchwork of different properties he had put
together. Among the projects that Millard undertook was to plant the
hillside that is now home to the Wild Garden.

Of that planting, little remains. When New York City took over Wave
Hill in 1960, before Stufano took charge, this area was subjected to a

This knot of cutleaf staghorn sumac (*Rhus typhina* 'Laciniata') is one of the few survivors from Albert Millard's early-20th-century planting of the area.

destructive maintenance regime. Abandoned for the rest of the year, the garden was invaded by Parks Department laborers in late July; they would turn the soil in the beds with spading forks just as rampant weeds were going to seed, essentially sowing the space with invasives. All that survived this treatment was a handful of die-hard irises, a knot of cutleaf staghorn sumac (*Rhus typhina* 'Laciniata'), and a cluster of overgrown yews.

The path system that Millard had designed, however, remained, as did a round gazebo he had built at the top of the hill. Stufano and Nally pragmatically preserved both in the new garden they designed.

Another survivor from the Wild Garden's previous incarnation, this nearly white iris (*Iris* 'Florentina') continues to bloom reliably every spring.

OPPOSITE, CLOCKWISE FROM TOP LEFT

Originally conceived as a collection of species-type plants, the Wild Garden has been infiltrated by irresistible cultivars that fit the garden's look, including species-type red columbine (*Aquilegia canadensis*), native to rocky slopes throughout eastern North America; a semi-double-flowered, purple columbine cultivar; a double-flowered pink columbine cultivar; and a purple-blue columbine cultivar.

WILLIAM ROBINSON

Stufano attributes the inspiration for the Wild Garden to the rugged, untamed nature of the site, and to the gardens that the famous landscape architectural firm Olmsted Brothers had designed for Fort Tryon Park. It's true that Fort Tryon is conveniently close at hand, just across the Spuyten Duyvil Creek from the Bronx in northern Manhattan. Yet it is also impossible to create any sort of landscape in this vein without referring back in some way to the work of the great Irish gardener William Robinson (1838–1935). The Olmsteds themselves were open about their debt to him. Robinson made a career as a horticultural iconoclast, contradicting and correcting the gardening traditions of his day.

His greatest accomplishment was his concept for a "wild garden." The prevalent design style of his era was one of bedding out, of arranging thousands of annual flowers in intricate geometrical patterns—a sort of gardener's paint by numbers. By contrast, Robinson's concept for a wild garden depended mainly on hardy, wild-type plants that could withstand local winters and perform in the garden as perennials. For these, the eclectic Robinson sourced from all over the world. He would introduce the widely procured plants into the garden and then let them find their own places.

In his manifesto, *The Wild Garden*, first published in 1870, Robinson wrote, "There has been some misunderstanding as to the term 'Wild Garden'. It is applied essentially to the placing of perfectly hardy exotic plants under conditions where they will thrive without further care."

Robinson prefigured modern-day tastes, although his emphasis on exotic flora over British plants would not please contemporary native-plant purists. In fact, he did include some invasive weeds, notably bindweed (*Convolvulus arvensis*), when he sought to demonstrate the depth of his principles in his own plantings at his estate in southern England, Gravetye Manor. Coincidentally, bindweed was a major pest at the site of the Wave Hill Wild Garden—Stufano had to blanket the soil with black plastic for two years to get rid of it.

Certainly, the biggest difference between Robinson's wild garden and the one at Wave Hill is one of scale. Whereas Gravetye Manor's wild garden took several of the estate's 1000 acres, Wave Hill's Wild Garden is barely a half acre. For Gelene Scarborough, the Wave Hill gardener responsible

for this area, the smaller size is an advantage. "This," she says, "is a New York City version, compressed into a smaller space. Which I love about it, because it makes for a really intense garden."

To give a true flavor of the wild places to which this garden pays tribute, Stufano and Nally decided to focus the planting on "straight species plants"—plants that had been taken straight from the wild and not tinkered with by plant breeders. This meant that they could not, for the most part, depend on nurseries as a source of supply, as nurseries typically traffic in hybrids and horticultural selections that differ in some respect—larger flowers, variegated foliage—from the wild population. Rather, they were obliged to resort to the seed-distribution programs of such bodies as Britain's Royal Horticultural Society and the Royal Botanic Gardens at Kew. In the days before the internet, finding seed of some desired species was a laborious process of poring through printed pamphlets. But Marco and John persisted.

Not all the plants in the Wild Garden follow this rule, however. Gelene Scarborough had the good fortune to begin working in the Wild Garden in 1997, under the supervision of John Emmanuel, who in turn had worked with Stufano and Nally in the Wild Garden's early days. Gelene wondered at the presence of many cultivars, horticultural selections, and "improved" plants, in this sanctuary for species. As Emmanuel explained, Marco and John were full of excitement at choosing plants for their first Wave Hill garden, in a fever of discovery at the time, and simply could not resist some of the cultivated plants they came across. Reasoning that this was not a botanical collection but rather a public garden, they saw no reason to exclude plants arbitrarily if they fit the look. As a result, some cultivars found a home there. The same ethic continues to this day.

And so this has always been, by design, a garden in flux. There is continuity in the basic structure. Conditions were varied in the different Wild Garden beds to create different kinds of habitats. There is, for example, a shady, slightly moist bed well enriched with compost, not far from a sun-drenched dry bed where the soil was mixed with sand to enhance its drainage. In this way, each bed offers an opportunity to grow a different type of plant. Scarborough has worked to preserve this mix—recently, she dug out and replaced the soil in the dry bed because the original mix had accumulated too much water-retaining humus over the years.

OPPOSITE, CLOCKWISE FROM TOP LEFT

Some of the Wild Garden's different habitats: A partially shaded woodland opening; woodland; hillside grassland; dry upland.

A shifting tapestry of plants—once plants are installed in suitable habitats, each finds its own place.

OPPOSITE

Blue camas (*Camassia leichtlinii* subsp. *suksdorfii*) and self-sown *Allium* species interweave in the Wild Garden in early May.

Overlaid on this structure of habitats is a shifting tapestry of plants. The philosophy in the Wild Garden has always been, once the plants are installed in suitable habitats, to let them find their own place. As a result, the placement of individual species continually changes as the various plants jostle for position and as the pattern of sunlight evolves. This last, the pattern of sunlight, has changed notably over the decades as the garden has matured. Some of the dwarf evergreens that were used to structure the beds have expanded to a considerable size, casting more shade every year. In the more than 40 years of the garden's existence, some have become so big that they no longer fit the scale of the compact space. These have been gradually removed, so that areas that were shaded have suddenly become sunny. In some places, deleted evergreens have been replaced with young specimens of the same type; in others, newer, improved cultivars have been substituted.

Threadleaf coreopsis (*Coreopsis verticillata*), front, and knautia (*Knautia macedonica*), center, add another layer in June, with a weeping Atlas cedar (*Cedrus atlantica* 'Glauca Pendula') in the background.

ABOVE RIGHT

July brings (front to back) sea holly (*Eryngium planum*), ornamental onion (*Allium tanguticum*), and globe thistle (*Echinops sphaerocephalus*).

OPPOSITE

Abyssinian gladiolus (*Gladiolus murielae*) hangs languorously over knautia and threadleaf coreopsis in August's plantscape.

Much of the Wild Garden's changeability reflects an emphasis on self-seeding annuals and biennials. As in the Flower Garden, these are allowed to set seed, and so self-propagate. Scarborough calculates that such self-seeders compose some 30 to 40 percent of the plants in the Wild Garden, adding that they play a somewhat different role there than in the Flower Garden. It is, in large part, the dense and tumultuous appearance of the plantings that inject the wild into the Wild Garden, and this appearance is largely the effect of the self-seeders inserting themselves into every vacancy. Of course, self-sowers also find their way into places where they are not wanted, such as paths and among the branches of shrubs, and so require energetic editing.

As the trees grow and spread their branches, patterns of light and shade shift, and the plants rearrange themselves.

More than 40 years after the first development of the Wild Garden, some of the evergreens have reached sizable height.

The Wild Garden

Some dwarf evergreens have, with decades of growth, become quite large, like this limber pine (*Pinus flexilis* 'Glauca Prostrata') at center; in some cases, they have had to be removed and replaced with smaller specimens, restarting the cycle.

The Wild Garden

FROM LEFT TO RIGHT

Self-seeding annuals and biennials, such as mullein (*Verbascum* species), rear left, and yellow foxglove (*Digitalis grandiflora*), front, compose 30 to 40 percent of the plants here, creating a dense and tousled appearance.

Hollyhocks (*Alcea rosea*) also find their way about the Wild Garden, their tall flower stalks providing vertical notes from early summer to midsummer.

Foxgloves (*Digitalis purpurea*), biennial imports from Europe, provide self-propagating grace notes.

OPPOSITE

Another self-sowing biennial, dyer's woad (*Isatis tinctoria*) furnishes thickets of yellow flowers in spring.

Despite William Robinson's assertion that a wild garden, once planted, would take care of itself, Gelene Scarborough's experience has been the exact opposite. The truth, she says, is that the lines of the composition are set in the arrangement of the shrubs, dwarf evergreens, and perennials. All the gardener can do is refine the picture. Yet that—refining by editing—plays a crucial role in the garden's success and occupies most of her time. She not only thins and removes plants, but moves them around as well. This activity poses a two-fold challenge, not only to restrain the too-prolific plants, but also to maintain just the right degree of wildness. The garden can't look too planned, despite the fact that getting the richest display requires a lot of planning. Equally, though, the opposite is true: the Wild Garden can't look too chaotic or it degenerates into a mere mess.

One of the most brilliant touches of this design is the manipulation of the view. The visitor enters the garden at its downhill side, necessarily facing away from the river. This pattern continues as you climb up the paths and through the beds, although there are a couple of turns that expose visitors for a moment to the picture of the broad waterway and the cliffs of the Palisades on the river's far side. But it isn't until you

Although the Wild Garden largely plants and replants itself, considerable editing is required to keep it at the right degree of spontaneity and prevent it from tipping into chaos.

OPPOSITE, CLOCKWISE FROM TOP LEFT

One of the entrances to the Wild Garden, a set of steps that passes under a rustic structure, is covered with trumpet vine (*Campsis radicans* f. *flava*).

This hilltop gazebo provides a climax to the walk.

A network of paths takes visitors up through the garden, revealing choice views at intentional intervals.

enter the gazebo and turn at the hill's top that you enjoy the full force of the vista. Even here the view is carefully presented. The overgrown yews that Stufano and Nally found here when they began the garden were clipped into something resembling heaps of green cushions, and these frame two vistas, one of the river and the other of a picturesque weeping cedar to the southwest.

A popular concept in gardening these days is that of layering. Consider the garden in terms of a series of planes: floor, shrub level, and tree canopy, say the advocates of this approach, planting to fill each. Then plant it, additionally, as a series of compositions succeeding each other in time—all the plants coexisting, but arranged so as to create attractive

Venerable yews, clipped into green, cushioned
mounds, frame the gazebo's views.

Clematis (*Clematis montana* var. *rubens*) has climbed this yew, lending a late-spring bloom to the normally somber evergreen.

pictures at different seasons. Thus, one layer emerges in spring, another in early summer, one in midsummer, and subsequent layers in late summer and autumn. Wave Hill's Wild Garden works in both these senses, spatial and temporal, and actually synthesizes the two kinds of layers.

Early spring is a low carpet of smaller bulbs and spring ephemerals. In April, in the bed visitors pass as they enter, windflower (*Anemone blanda*) from southeastern Europe

and the Caucasus partners with Corsican hellebores (*Helleborus lividus* subsp. *corsicus*), campernelle jonquils (*Narcissus ×odorus*, a naturally occurring hybrid of a Spanish-Portuguese species), striped squills (*Puschkinia scilloides* var. *libanotica*, from the Middle East), and species tulips from Crete, Turkey, Bulgaria, and Greece.

The effect is of a pan-Mediterranean upland, but this is rapidly replaced by a taller, more meadowlike layer of large camas (*Camassia leichtlinii* subsp. *suksdorfii*), foxtail lily (*Eremurus himalaicus*), celandine poppy (*Stylophorum diphyllum*), and others. The garden continues in this vein until, by October, it has become a pocket prairie of tall Chinese silver grasses (*Miscanthus sinensis* 'Gracillimus', 'Silver Feather', and 'Variegatus') and giant reed (*Arundo donax*) decorated in part with late-flowering asters (*Symphyotrichum oblongifolium* 'October Skies' and *Symphyotrichum novae-angliae* 'Our Latest One'), South African foxglove (*Ceratotheca triloba*), and the vining Spanish flag (*Ipomoea lobata*), which despite its common name is actually a native of Brazil.

Piling layer on layer in this fashion not only provides a succession of bloom throughout the growing season, it keeps transforming the topography of the garden so that no two visits present the same aspect. Even the

The flower spires of foxtail lilies, as much as 20 to 33 inches long, are spectacular in season, but after the bloom, this plant goes dormant, retreating back underground in midsummer.

OPPOSITE

White-flowering dogwood trees bloom as Virginia bluebells and narcissus retreat and tall, late-season perennials emerge.

ABOVE

Woodland tulips
(Tulipa sylvestris).

OPPOSITE, CLOCKWISE FROM TOP LEFT

One of the spring ephemerals, shooting star (*Dodecatheon meadia*), blooms in May then
goes dormant, hiding underground through the summer; hybrid windflower (*Anemone ×lip-siensis*) also follows the spring ephemerals' schedule, bearing pale-yellow flowers in
April; checkered lily (*Fritillaria meleagris*); a shy but graceful ornament of early spring to
midspring is *Fritillaria pallida*.

Dark-flowered tulips and pink honesty (*Lunaria Annua*, lower left) contrast with yellow basket-of-gold (*Aurinia saxatilis*) in spring.

RIGHT

Wild columbine, irises, and a soft-pink azalea (*Rhododendron* 'Colin Kendrick') in spring.

Asters (*Symphyotrichum* species) and fleece flower (*Persicaria amplexicaulis* 'Summer Dance') bloom as the foliage of the sumac turns color.

OPPOSITE, TOP

The old cutleaf staghorn sumac presides over polygonum, grasses, and asters in October.

OPPOSITE, BOTTOM

Grasses and white-flowered *Allium tuberosum* add a touch of gossamer to the Wild Garden in late summer.

vistas within the garden change as the plants in many beds grow up to screen or frame views, while other beds are purposely kept low-growing to preserve open views across them. Because you can't see around all the corners, the garden, when you are in it, feels much larger than it is.

People can be confused by a visit to this garden, thinking that because it's a wild garden it's just been let go. In fact, it's one of the most intensely maintained areas of Wave Hill. Having so many things growing together requires a lot of editing and moving and keeping things from swamping each other. What Scarborough does here, she says is "like painting in reverse." Yet, she loves the diversity and tumult of this garden. "You could work here your entire life and not feel bored."

The Wild Garden

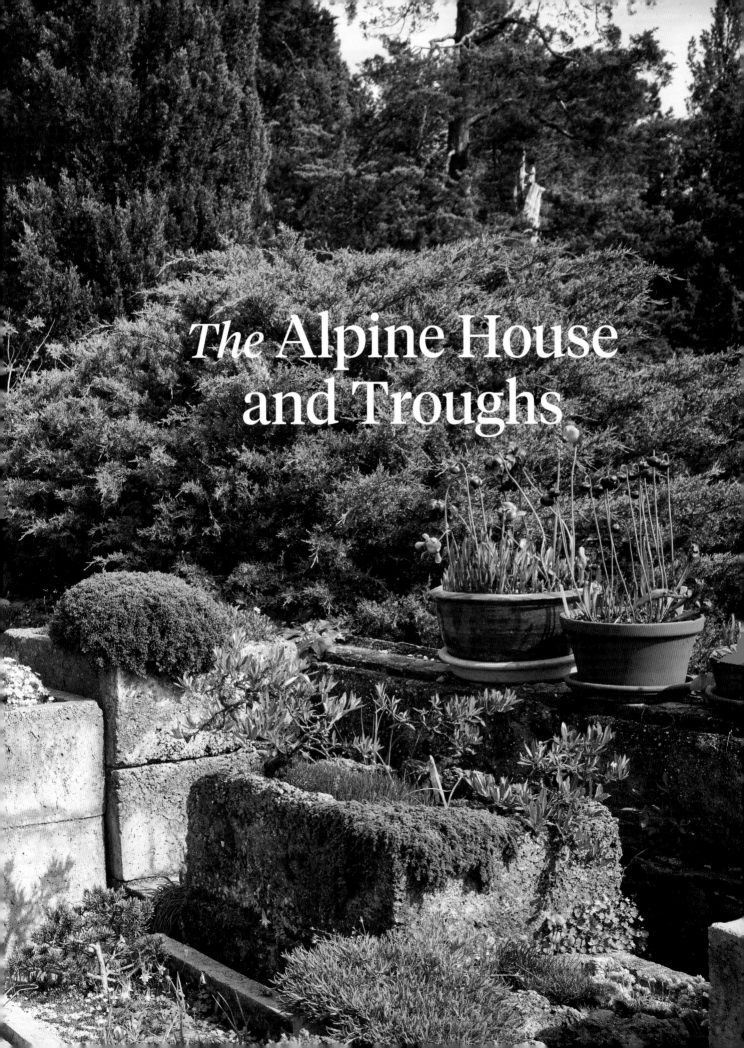

The Alpine House and Troughs

PREVIOUS SPREAD

Hypertufa troughs on the terrace in front of the Alpine House.

OPPOSITE

A fine display of miniatures on the terrace in front of Wave Hill's T.H. Everett Alpine House: a chir pine (*Pinus roxburghii*), center, presides over a Cyprus cedar (*Cedrus brevifolia* 'Treveron'), left, a Korean fir (*Abies koreana* 'Cis'), right, and a pincushion flower (*Scabiosa japonica* var. *alpina* 'Ritz Blue'), lower left.

The experience is like a museum visit. You stand before the crystal case, admiring the small, exquisite objects carefully arranged inside. But this is no trip to a gallery in Manhattan; it's a foray to the Bronx to visit Wave Hill's T.H. Everett Alpine House.

An interest in alpine plants—plants from the high mountains found naturally at or above the tree line—was something Marco Polo Stufano developed as a student at the New York Botanical Garden. These plants, which have evolved compact, highly structured forms so that they can tuck themselves into the shelter of rock crevices, are hard to grow outside their native terrain. They need a nutrient-poor mineral soil like that found on the peaks, one with a porous, fast-draining structure. They also require a deep root-run so that they can tap subsurface reservoirs of moisture while their crowns remain dry. Otherwise, these plants rot—especially during cold weather, a soggy soil is fatal to them. Adapted as they are to a nutritionally impoverished habitat, these plants are also slow growing. Their tight cushions of foliage may expand by as little as a quarter-inch a year. And though they typically demand full sunlight, they do not tolerate heat well, especially the humid heat found at midsummer in coastal, lowland New York City.

At the New York Botanical Garden, the alpine plants were, during Stufano's student days, grown in pit houses, low glasshouses set atop four-foot-deep chambers excavated into the soil. This design eliminated the need for winter heating. Heat transferred from the subsoil, combined with the solar radiation absorbed through the roof, kept the interior warm enough for the chill-hardy alpines. In summer, these sunken chambers stayed somewhat cooler than their surroundings, helping to ease the alpines through the seasonal heat. However, although the pit houses enabled the cultivation of alpines, they didn't provide a venue

The Alpine House and Troughs

for public viewing. Accordingly, these plants remained one of the private passions of Marco's mentor, T.H. Everett, the director of horticulture at the New York Botanical Garden.

It was after graduation, though, during his first trip to Britain in 1965, that Stufano saw what a properly appointed display for alpines could be. During this trip he visited the specially constructed alpine houses at the Royal Botanic Garden, Kew, at the edge of London, and at the Royal Botanic Garden in Edinburgh, Scotland. In Edinburgh, he also viewed another means of growing alpines, purpose-built masonry troughs arranged in an outdoor setting.

Marco returned with a plan to create something similar at Wave Hill. In 1983, after he and his staff completed the Herb and Dry Garden (see following chapter), he raised sufficient funds to cap that hillside with a specially designed alpine house (named in honor of his mentor). Removable glass and plastic roof and wall panels help insure that the interior of the structure does not overheat; a sand-filled "bench," a waist-high table topped with six inches of coarse sand, provides a cool medium into which to plunge the bottoms of alpine-containing pots, keeping the roots from overheating.

Even with this facility, however, cultivating alpines successfully required special measures. To accommodate their deep roots, alpine plants are planted in pots call "Long Toms," extra-tall terra-cotta pots. The potting mix replicates the nutrient-poor, gritty soil found in the mountains, although with a few extra ingredients. For instance, bonemeal is included to provide a slow, modest feed of phosphate, which fosters strong root growth, an important factor for the deep-rooted alpines. Lime provides calcium and helps balance the soil's pH. Grit, specifically the crushed rock sold as grower grit for poultry at feed stores, enhances the drainage of the soil. Charcoal helps to prevent anaerobic decay of

OPPOSITE

Sharp-lobed hepatica (*Hepatica acutiloba*) marks earliest spring with its blue blossoms.

BELOW

A pale-colored specimen of Auricula primrose (*Primula auricula*) 'Blue Velvet' nestled into its Long Tom.

Wave Hill's Alpine Soil Mix

Note: A 2-gallon bucket is used as a measuring tool; home gardeners may wish to reduce amounts proportionately.

2 buckets of loam

2 buckets of sphagnum peat

2 buckets of perlite

2½ buckets of grit

1 bucket of vermiculite

1 bucket of sand

½ bucket of charcoal

½ cup of lime

3 cups of bonemeal

the organic matter, and so keeps the soil from souring. This is especially important with the slow-growing alpines, which may spend a year or more in the same soil before repotting.

Watering the plants in the Alpine House is a daily chore in the summer, although a much less frequent one in winter. To guard against dehydration, the gardeners also moisten the sand in the bench, so that when the soil in the pots dries, moisture can migrate in through their terra-cotta walls.

Fertilization is minimal, as such slow-growing plants do not need, and, in fact, cannot cope with, a flood of nutrients. In early spring, the plants receive a dilute application of a water-soluble, balanced fertilizer with micronutrients, just as they come out of dormancy. Thereafter, fertilizing is based on the needs of the individual plant, applied when growth starts. When plants are coming into bloom, a switch is made to a formula higher in phosphate and potassium (3-12-16) to enhance the flowering.

Even with this special care, there is only a relatively small group of true high-mountain plants that can withstand the combined heat and humidity of a New York City summer. For this reason, the gardeners at Wave Hill have relaxed the definition of an "alpine" to include other plants, which, although they may not originate at high altitude, are compatible in both their appearance and their cultural needs. "Small, low, and slow" is Louis Bauer's succinct definition of what the Wave Hill staff looks for in these alpine companions. They have to survive in the lean soils preferred by the high-mountain plants, they have to be compact so that they will not overshadow their neighbors, and they must grow slowly enough that they won't crowd out the true alpines.

Water sweating out through porous walls and evaporating off the surface of the hypertufa keeps the troughs cool even on this sunny August day.

There are a number of genetically dwarfed evergreen shrubs and trees, such as the Japanese holly (*Ilex* 'Rock Garden'), which over a period of 15 years typically reaches a height of only six to 12 inches, with a spread of perhaps twice the height. Likewise, the eastern white pine cultivar *Pinus strobus* 'Horsford' contents itself with a height and spread of one foot.

An inhabitant of another kind of challenging habitat, dwarf statice (*Limonium minutum*) naturally grows in crevices of limestone cliffs overlooking the sea in southeastern France; it shares the nestling form of the true alpines, making a compact cushion of fleshy leaves six to eight inches across. Another plant of high altitude, from the shoulders of the Rocky Mountains, Kelsey's phlox (*Phlox kelseyi*) fits the profile: it forms

A bird's-eye view of miniature trough landscapes with fleabane (*Erigeron* species), bottom, and columbine (*Aquilegia* species), top.

ABOVE RIGHT

Dark blue blossoms of a seed-grown columbine (*Aquilegia* species) preside over this stepped assemblage of troughs.

OPPOSITE

A mosslike dianthus (*Dianthus simulans*) spills over the edge of this container, contrasting with the yellow blossoms of creeping broom (*Genista pilosa*) and the peach and green foliage of a perennial geranium (*Geranium* species).

a dense six-inch mound of foliage that covers itself with bluish lavender in early spring.

As a rule, the alpines, accustomed as they are to cool temperatures, awaken early, so that by April their glasshouse is full of blossoms and the display of colors peaks in May. The unique attraction of these plants, however—what sets them apart from the rest of Wave Hill's flora—is their remarkably architectural form. The neatly sculpted mounds, globes, and pillows of foliage that they make, the petite ground-hugging carpets, the gnarled branches of the miniature shrubs, hold the allure of any miniature. Looking at them laid out in the sand, the urge to start your own collection is nearly irresistible.

Just how the average gardener without a glasshouse can maintain an alpine collection is shown on the terrace immediately fronting the Alpine House. Here, piled atop one another like children's blocks, are rectangular, rough-walled troughs. Constructed on site from a special concrete mix (hypertufa) that mimics the appearance of tufa, the common name for a type of porous volcanic rock, these containers serve as homes for downsized landscapes of alpines and dwarf evergreens.

They are well suited to keeping these demanding plants healthy. When filled with alpine potting mix, the hypertufa troughs offer near-perfect drainage: water can escape through the porous walls of the troughs, as well as through the drainage holes in the bottom. The Wave Hill gardeners have further enhanced this effect by making their larger, stationary troughs bottomless; their undersides are plugged only with rectangles of concrete-reinforcing wire mesh topped with nylon screening to keep the potting mix from washing out. This feature is what also allows the gardeners to stack these troughs one on top of another, creating an extra-deep root run for the plants.

The porosity of the troughs' walls not only serves as an escape for excess water, it also serves as a rudimentary climate-control system. The moisture that sweats out through the walls evaporates off the troughs' surface on sunny days, helping to keep the troughs, and the plants inside them, cool.

Typically, container plantings are envisioned as living equivalents of cut-flower displays, and are designed as such. Trough plantings, however, function as complete, if diminutive, landscapes, with the tiny cushions and carpets of the alpines, and dwarf evergreens, standing in for the shrubs and trees of a regular garden.

Susannah Strazzera, the gardener currently in charge of the Alpine House, has taken this mimicry a step further, sometimes planting troughs with regional themes. Examples are one trough planted entirely with flora from the Rocky Mountain West, another with Japanese miniatures such as dragon's head (*Dracocephalum argunense*) and a dwarf false cypress (*Chamaecyparis* cultivar).

Most of the troughs, however, were created just to satisfy the aesthetic preferences of the designer. Herein lies the special appeal of trough gardens, in particular for those with limited space at their command. Troughs can, and do, live on apartment balconies. Squat

OPPOSITE

A dwarf willow (*Salix repens* 'Boyd's Pendula') casts a gnarled shadow on the trough wall. In the background, a Chinese juniper (*Juniperus chinensis* 'Shimpaku'), top center, provides an evergreen note, while a moss phlox (*Phlox subulata*) blooms to the left. Below left is a dwarf pinyon pine (*Pinus edulis* 'Farmy').

BELOW

A globe daisy (*Globularia* species), top, and candytuft (*Iberis taurica*), below, present a perennial garden in miniature.

Build an Alpine Trough

Materials

Trough concrete mixture (see accompanying recipe)

Wheelbarrow

Bucket (for measuring materials)

Sieve (to screen peat moss)

Small shovel or hoe

Wire brush with metal scraper

Plastic trash bags

Rubber gloves

Mask

Trough forms: laundry baskets, plastic pots, cardboard boxes, etc.

Trough concrete mixture

Note: A 2-gallon bucket is used as a measuring tool.

1 bucket Portland cement (dark color, if available)

1 bucket coarse perlite

⅔ bucket peat moss, sieved to remove twigs and lumps

1 handful fiber mesh (available at masonry supply stores)

Water

1. Combine the dry materials for trough concrete mixture until thoroughly mixed. Add water a little at a time and mix with the hoe or shovel until the mixture resembles coarse oatmeal.

2. Immediately after the concrete has been mixed, line the trough form—pot, basket, or cardboard box—with a thick trash bag, making sure that the plastic overlaps the edges of the container by at least six inches.

3. Add the concrete mixture to the interior of the form a handful at a time, building up a bottom that is about two inches thick. Make sure that each new handful firmly attaches to the last one, so that no weak spots or pockets are created.

4. Once the bottom is in place, build up the side walls of the trough by adding handfuls of concrete mixture to the inside of the walls of the form. The side walls of the trough should be at least one and a half inches thick and should extend all the way to the top of the form.

Again, press handfuls of concrete mix together firmly to prevent weak spots and pockets.

5. Poke one or two drainage holes in the bottom of the trough with a dowel.

6. Enclose the form and trough in a plastic bag overnight.

7. The next day, remove the form from the plastic bag and test the firmness of the concrete. If the concrete has set up hard, tug at the plastic bag lining of the form to loosen it. When the plastic and trough are loosened, invert the form carefully onto a flat surface.

8. Lift the form off the trough. Remove the plastic bag from the trough and reopen drainage holes with a large nail.

9. To remove the wrinkles left by the plastic bag and create a more natural appearance, brush the entire trough, inside and out, with a wire brush. If desired, shape the edges of the trough (carefully) with the scraper on the wire brush's end.

10. Return the trough to the plastic bag and let it cure for four to six weeks. After that time, remove the trough from the bag and use a propane torch to carefully burn off any protruding bits of fiber mesh.

11. Leave the trough outdoors to weather for three to four months so that excess lime will leach out of the concrete before you fill the trough with potting mix and plant.

down and go eye-to-eye with one, and be transported from cityscape to pristine mountainside. Some of the plants play with the sense of scale, the tiny buns and shoots bearing normal-sized flowers when they bloom. Others produce blossoms as delicate as the foliage, snapping the viewer back into miniscule.

The care of the troughs is similar to that of the plants inside the Alpine House, except that they receive a dose of fish emulsion in early spring (when mountain plants

Crevices in a mortarless, dry-laid stone wall also provide hospitable spots for alpines and their companions. Upper left, dianthus; center, columbine; bottom right, forget-me-not.

A succulent, cobweb hen and chicks (*Sempervivum arachnoideum*), flourishes in the perfect drainage of the alpine wall.

Echoing the scenery of the distant Hudson River Palisades, the troughs present a vista of miniature cliffs.

Jonquils (*Narcissus jonquilla*) combine with *Oxalis obtusa* 'Tangerine' and grape hyacinth (*Muscari neglectum*) to brighten an early April day in the Alpine House. Though not a native of high mountains, jonquils like fast-draining soils and cool conditions, making them compatible with true alpines.

customarily receive a burst of nutrients from snow melt) as well as the regular regimen of water-soluble fertilizers. Because the reservoir of soil is larger, the troughs do not need watering as frequently, especially when natural rainfall supplements what falls from the watering can. For those who vacation in summertime, when alpines in conventional pots may need irrigation every day, troughs are a more workable option.

Visitors ooh and aah over the Alpine House, but what they more typically identify with, and imagine themselves creating, are the troughs. Not on a Wave Hill–scale surely, but almost anyone can find a sunny spot for one or two of the miniature landscapes. They have the appeal of bonsai, the impact of a larger garden distilled into an essential minimum. Just the right size, in short, for some of nature's most exquisite creations.

Hybrid camellia (*Camellia* 'Crimson Candles') thrives in the consistently cool, but not frigid, winter temperatures of the Alpine House, rewarding visitors with an early-spring bloom.

ABOVE LEFT

Native to arid regions of South Africa, *Oxalis obtusa* 'Tangerine' nevertheless fits Bauer's requirements of "small, slow, and low," and shares the alpines' preference for fast-draining soil.

Tucked in behind the Alpine House is this back-door vignette of potted miniature trees: dwarf Caucasian fir (*Abies nordman-niana* 'Golden Spreader'), top; Chinese fringe flower (*Loropetalum chinense* 'Rubrum'), bottom left; and a Japanese maple (*Acer palmatum* cultivar), bottom right.

RIGHT

Burying the pot bottoms in six inches of coarse sand keeps the alpine plants' roots cool and provides a reservoir of moisture on which they can draw.

The Herb and
Dry Gardens

PREVIOUS SPREAD

Set into a south-facing slope, the Herb
Garden (front) and the Dry Garden (back),
enjoy the benefits of a warm, airy, and
well-drained microclimate.

BELOW

The original 1920s-era glasshouses on this
site grew out-of-season vegetables, fruits,
and flowers for the household.

L ouis Bauer describes these as "ruin gardens," and they certainly are
that. After all, along with everything else that Wave Hill's new staff
inherited when the estate passed into the hands of New York City were
the derelict glasshouses. Standing on a south-facing slope, these had been
used to grow out-of-season vegetables and flowers for the estate's owners,
but by the 1970s nothing remained except stone foundations topped with
decaying frames and broken panes of glass. Inside, labyrinths of concrete
paths divided beds of neglected, barren soil. The transformation of this
dreary scene into elegant complexes of plantings was an outstanding
example of creative reuse. In addition, though, it was, and is, a virtuoso
demonstration of horticultural ingenuity.

When the glass and superstructures were cleared away, the foundations
were left intact. The lower one served first as an impromptu composting
facility; vegetable debris was dumped within the foundation to decay.
Later, for a couple of years, pumpkins were grown there. The vines,
expansive leaves, and fruits sprawled across
the paths; heat-loving plants flourished in
the semi-enclosed, south-facing space. The
beds, elevated between the walls of the former
foundations and set on a slope, also provided
perfect drainage and an airy spot. These facts
proved an inspiration.

In part, Marco Polo Stufano wanted to maintain
Wave Hill's lineage as a private estate and
include in the new gardens a tribute to the sort of
utilitarian plants that had once been grown for
the benefit of the household. But the conditions
within the old glasshouses—hot, dry in the

summer, and sun-drenched with poorish soil—also suggested certain types of plants.

Climate and soil are the two basic facts of any garden. You can apply all the care you want, but if you don't select plants appropriate to the climate and soil of your site, your garden will fail. That said, ingenious gardeners can often accomplish the unexpected by exploiting the peculiarities of their plot. Sometimes a trick of the topography will create a microclimate, a restricted area in which the prevailing climate differs significantly from that of its surroundings. Likewise, as in the former glasshouse beds, there may be pockets of distinctive soil.

With the glasshouses demolished, one foundation served for several years as impromptu compost bins.

The two stone enclosures on the south-facing hill had created twin rectangles of a Mediterranean type of climate: dry and warm to hot in the summer, with relatively mild, wetter winters. Such a climate is found naturally in many parts of the world besides the Mediterranean basin. It occurs as well in most of California, in parts of western and south Australia, in southwestern South Africa, regions of western and central Asia and in central Chile. For a plant collector, these are regions of great interest because they commonly support an outstanding diversity of vegetation. This is especially true of South Africa and California; the Mediterranean basin itself is host to a disproportionate share of the aromatic shrubs, subshrubs, and herbs that make up our culinary flavorings.

THE HERB GARDEN

In fact, such a microclimate is ideal for an herb garden, and Stufano set to work installing one in the lower of the two foundations. He disturbed the existing situation as little as possible, leaving the former glasshouses' concrete paths in place (eventually these were resurfaced with bluestone), and didn't even upgrade the soil in the old beds. The poor quality of this unimproved soil was actually an advantage, for herbs as a group make their thriftiest growth on lean, gritty, nutrient-poor soils—richer soils prompt them to outgrow themselves and flop.

Designed for teaching, the Herb Garden is the most methodical and highly structured of Wave Hill's plantings. The beds are divided by

Maximizing Microclimates

Wave Hill's varied terrain graces it with an abundance of microclimates. There are endless nooks and corners with different exposures to sunlight and the wind, with reflected heat from adjacent walls, or shade from overhanging trees. It's one of the garden's great resources. Visitors constantly remark on the diversity of plants to be found at Wave Hill. The key is the number of microclimates, offering a variety of growing conditions.

Focusing on microclimates is another way of interpreting the gardening rule of right plant, right place—finding a plant adapted to the conditions of the spot is the secret of successful growing. Often, of course, a desire for a certain look or a lust for rarities may persuade a gardener to insert a particular plant where it is not inclined to flourish. Extra nurturing may enable the misplaced plant to survive, but mere survival is no substitute for the vigorous growth that is essential to an attractive garden.

To find just the right plant for each spot requires a sensitivity to microclimates. "Be observant," urges Louis Bauer. "Look and feel like a plant. Because they are very sensitive to little variations." Recognizing differences in the exposure to sunlight is fundamental but also relatively easy, as our eyes automatically register differences in the strength of the light. This could be further quantified by keeping notes on sunlight and shadow at the time of the solstice versus that of the equinox. Other characteristics may be less obvious to the human observer but no less important to the plants. Is the site open to the breeze and therefore inclined to dry out faster? Or is it an enclosed pocket where the humidity tends to linger? Is there an adjacent wall or rock

An example of capitalizing on a microclimate is the lavender collection. Planted along the western side of Wave Hill's gift shop and visitor center, it benefits from the building's reflected heat and light and the warmth they bring.

The Herb and Dry Gardens

that absorbs and re-radiates solar energy, boosting the average temperature of the microclimate? Is the soil sandy, quick to drain and dry out, or does it retain the moisture, providing a damp foundation to the spot?

Microclimates can also be created. The walls, pergolas, and evergreens that have been erected or planted at Wave Hill over the years not only provide three-dimensional structure and focal points, they also, each of them, create their own complex of unique conditions. The lavender border, for example, that edges a path along the western side of Wave Hill's Perkins Visitor Center benefits from the effects of that building, installed more than a decade ago. Reflected heat and light from the buildings and pavement enhance the warmth of that area, and a relatively thin soil suits lavender, a subshrub native to rocky Mediterranean hillsides.

Providing a variety of experiences is essential to maintaining the interest of a garden, and thanks to its many microclimates, Wave Hill has a plenitude. "It feels different," Bauer contends, "when you walk into those different microclimates. You have a corner for this and an open spot for that and a shaded corner or something else. And it feels especially different when they are planted with appropriate plants."

In an ingenious example of creative repurposing, the former glasshouse foundations were recycled as the frames for the Herb and Dry Gardens.

barriers of slate into 88 two-foot-by-two-foot squares. Planted in them are the broadest assortment of useful plants, including culinary herbs such as fennel (*Foeniculum vulgare*) and garden thyme (*Thymus vulgaris*), medicinal plants such as foxglove (*Digitalis purpurea*), fruits such as figs (*Ficus carica*) and pomegranate (*Punica granatum*), fiber plants such as cotton (*Gossypium herbaceum*) and flax (*Linum usitatissimum*), and even herbs once used to dye cloths, such as Chinese indigo (*Persicaria*

tinctoria) and dyer's broom (*Cytisus tinctoria*). As a former student of painting, Gelene Scarborough, the gardener assigned to this area, is particularly interested in the dye plants.

The art in planning a garden of this sort lies in making it aesthetically pleasing as well as educational. That was particularly challenging in this case, where the setting was comprised of such severely rectilinear beds, divided so precisely in a monotonous series of identical squares. Scarborough looked at it as an engaging puzzle. Herbs were selected on the basis of attractiveness as much as utility. The center of the garden was planted as a focal point around which the rest could rotate, a squared arrangement of four small carpets of garden thyme backed by globes of boxwood (*Buxus sinica* var. *insularis* 'Justin Brouwers'). Then the more imposing, structural plants were arranged, such as vetiver (*Chrysopogon zizanioides*), lemon grass (*Cymbopogon citratus*), bay laurel (*Laurus nobilis*), and olive (*Olea europaea*) trees.

The focal point of the Herb Garden is a four-square composition of boxwoods (*Buxus sinica* var. *insularis* 'Justin Brouwers') set into garden thyme (*Thymus vulgaris*).

OPPOSITE

View through the Herb Garden to the Dry Garden above and the T.H. Everett Alpine House.

Among the structural plants are flowering herbs such as borage (*Borago officinalis*) and marsh mallow (*Althaea officinalis*). The slate frames help to confine the more aggressive spreaders, a common liability among herbs. Early bloomers that flame out with the arrival of summer heat, such as milk thistle (*Silybum marianum*), are replaced with tropicals such as cardamom (*Elettaria cardamomum*). Self-seeders such as clary sage (*Salvia sclarea*) and poppies (*Papaver* species) were previously allowed to scatter themselves through the beds to instill a sense of unity, but these interjections confused visitors seeking to learn the identity of the plants in each bed, so the self-sowers were reined in.

Containers punctuate the beds sparingly. Ornamental peppers might be the theme one summer, or perhaps nasturtiums. Cup and saucer vine (*Cobaea scandens*) clothes the arch over an entrance. Foliage textures necessarily play a large part in a garden of plants that are commonly

The Herb and Dry Gardens

The Herb Garden, southwest corner.

grown for the useful properties of their leaf tissues. Large-fingered leaves of golden seal (*Hydrastis canadensis*) set off the lacy mound of a neighboring parsley (*Petroselinum crispum*); the fuzzy, fleshy leaves of Mexican mint (*Plectranthus amboinicus*) look all the softer when juxtaposed with spiky fuller's teasel (*Dipsacus fullonum*).

Because the herbs were not selected on the basis of a similarity of origin, they do include a few plants not as well adapted to the conditions in the old glasshouse foundation. There is sweet basil (*Ocimum basilicum*), for example, turmeric (*Curcuma longa*), and lemon grass, all natives of tropical Asia, which require supplemental watering to flourish here. Overhead watering with sprinklers didn't work, as what was adequate irrigation for the tropicals proved too much for such dryland plants as

Containers punctuate the Herb Garden, planted to a different theme every summer.

ABOVE LEFT

The east side of the Herb Garden, with an old glasshouse entrance converted into a niche with a bench. An arch draped with cup-and-saucer vine (*Cobaea scandens*) shades the resting spot.

the thymes. Hand watering has been employed, but fortunately isn't needed very often, because so many of the herbs come from dryish climates and are drought resistant.

THE DRY GARDEN

A different tack was taken in the foundation higher on the slope. Here a plan was developed to take full advantage of the microclimate and grow plants that wouldn't flourish elsewhere on the grounds, or even elsewhere in the region. Dubbed the Dry Garden, this was to focus on a collection of ornamental plants from Mediterranean-type climates. Envisioned before the birth of the xeriscaping movement, this planting exhibits a similar plant palette, but the garden was designed not so much to cope with dry conditions as to enhance and celebrate them.

Previous to this planting, many of the species here were considered unable to weather a New York winter. Autumn sage (*Salvia greggii*), for instance, although a fully perennial shrub in its native southern Texas and Mexico, is typically short-lived in the northeastern states. It commonly overwinters successfully in this garden, as does rosemary (*Rosmarinus officinalis*), which in New York must typically spend the

winter indoors. Likewise, ice plant (*Delosperma cooperi*), a succulent, evergreen ground cover from South Africa, though much planted in the American Southwest, was considered a poor prospect to survive a winter outdoors in New York. This unfortunate presumption was often wrongly attributed to a simple sensitivity to cold. What the Wave Hill staff discovered, however, was that the fatal factor for such plants was the *combination* of freezing and wet: the roots, adapted as they were to drier climates, would rot when subjected to those dual conditions. However, in the quick-draining soil of Wave Hill's Dry Garden, many of the supposedly non-hardy plants overwinter successfully.

Initially, the gardeners relied just on the topography of the site—the raised enclosure perched on a hill—to provide the drainage, and the results were adequate. In 2015, though, Gelene Scarborough addressed the soil. Digging the beds to a depth of two feet, she mixed the existing soil half and half with compost to enhance its drainage and provide some modest fertility, then topped all the beds with a six-inch layer of fine gravel, so that the crowns of the plants would also remain dry. At the same time, she rehabilitated the soil in the Herb Garden, mixing in compost as well as loam that she had first pasteurized by heating it to 180°F for a half-hour to kill any weed seeds. In retrospect, she believes the pasteurization of the soil was a mistake, as it exterminated its micro-flora and fauna, which has had long-term effects on the soil's vitality and structure. Neither the Dry nor the Herb Garden, incidentally, receive any fertilizer, since both classes of plants thrive on nutrient-poor soils.

Winter is one challenge, but New York's sultry summers are also difficult for the Dry Garden's plants. Typically, such dryland specimens have deep and extensive root systems that are expert at foraging for moisture, enabling them to shrug off summer heat and drought. Here, though, the plants' roots are confined to the relatively narrow run of the old glasshouse beds. This

OPPOSITE, CLOCKWISE FROM TOP LEFT

Lettuce serves as a foliage plant in this Herb Garden bed; grasses such as purple fountain grass (*Pennisetum setaceum* 'Rubrum') contribute texture and color; orange-tinted sulfur cosmos (*Cosmos sulphureus* 'Tango') surround a pot of curled-leaf parsley (*Petroselinum crispum*) at the Herb Garden's front; a cactus (*Opuntia humifusa*) thrives in a hot, dry, south-facing corner along a wall above the Herb Garden.

BELOW

A few steps above the Herb Garden, the Dry Garden was installed to take maximum advantage of the microclimate for the benefit of plants from Mediterranean climates.

means that during summer dry spells the plants, adapted to drought though they are, may occasionally need watering. The gravel mulch speeds the absorption of water into the beds, however, and the exposed, breezy nature of the site ensures that the above-ground portions of the plants dry rapidly. That makes it possible to irrigate this garden with sprinklers. An additional benefit of the gravel mulch, of course, is that it greatly reduces evaporation of water from the soil surface, and so reduces moisture loss from the beds.

As with the Herb Garden below it, the goal of the Dry Garden is not just to have the plants survive, but also to present them in an attractive way. Here the plants, which tend to be less aggressive than the herbs, are allowed to intermingle. Large structural choices, such as yuccas, junipers, and lavenders, were placed first. Then the perennials such as sages were arranged. Unlike in the Herb Garden, self-seeding annuals are a valued presence here. Dwarf zinnias (native to Mexico and Central America) pop up here and there, as do Mexican prickly poppies (*Argemone mexicana*). Sweet William silene (*Silene armeria*), a native of southern Europe, flourishes and also sows itself here, as does the rock pink (*Phemeranthus calycinus*), a native of the south-central and southwestern United States.

There is a steady menu of bloom here, from species tulips (natives of grasslands and mountainsides from southern Europe to central Asia) to summer-flowering lavenders, yuccas, and torch lilies (*Kniphofia* species, natives of South Africa), on into the fall with salvias (mostly from the American Southwest) and pink muhlygrass (*Muhlenbergia capillaris*, native to the western and central United States). But the dominating presence here, even more so than in the Herb Garden, is the foliage, and the key note is silver. Plants from a hot, dry climate tend to have silver foliage because silver functions like a mirror, reflecting sunlight and preventing overheating and dehydration. The differences in foliage colors can be subtle but still noticeable, ranging from the pewter silver of the lavenders (*Lavandula* species) and lavender cottons (*Santolina* species), to the bluish grays and green-grays of the moon carrot (*Seseli gummiferum*), the California fuchsia (*Epilobium canum* 'Chaparral Silver'), and the various sages (*Salvia* species).

There are other foliage colors here, as well: the rich, green leaves of the purple passionflower (*Passiflora incarnata*), the deep greens of the hardy

OPPOSITE

A California poppy (*Eschscholzia californica* 'Candy Kiss'). Reseeders are encouraged in the Dry Garden.

Foliage textures play the principal role in the Dry Garden.

OPPOSITE, TOP

Junipers (*Juniperus* species) have been used to structure the Dry Garden's display.

OPPOSITE, BOTTOM

Soft textures such as those of these Mexican feather grasses (*Nassella tenuissima*) and lavandin (*Lavandula ×intermedia* 'Grosso') contribute a tactile feel to this garden.

ice plant (*Delosperma sutherlandii*) and the common jasmine (*Jasminum officinale*), which fills the garden with perfume when it blooms in June. But the default is some shade of silver, which means that drama comes from the juxtaposition of different textures. The contrast of the bold, blade-shaped leaves of the yuccas with the fernlike leaves of yarrow (*Achillea filipendulina* 'Schwellenburg'); the ovate leaves of St. John's wort (*Hypericum tomentosum*) opposed to the needled foliage of the lavenders; the dissected leaves of the moon carrot and the long, fine, tufted leaves of pink muhlygrass.

Another aspect of the textures here is their softness. A few, such as the prickly junipers and the harsh yuccas, repel touch, but many more

ABOVE

Native purple passionflower (*Passiflora incarnata*), front left, climbs the foundation at the entrance to the Dry Garden.

OPPOSITE

Purple passionflower's unique blossom.

Early autumn in the Dry Garden.

invite it with a downy or felted surface. This reflects another adaptation to drought: such a coat of hairs shades the plant tissues underneath, helping to keep them cool. The quality of the hairs varies: horned poppies (*Glaucium flavum*) bristle, while the Hidalgo stachys (*Stachys albotomentosa*) has a shorter nap, and the lavender cottons (*Santolina chamaecyparissus*, *S. pinnata* 'Edward Bowles', and *S. rosmarinifolia*) have the wispy look that their common name suggests.

Another of the special pleasures of this garden is the assortment of fragrances. They invite you to close your eyes and inhale deeply, for many of the dryland plants saturate their foliage with aromatic oils—to ward off hungry insects and grazing animals, ecologists believe. The effect on the human nose, though, is appealing, whether it is the clean scent of the lavenders and lavender cottons or the fruity fragrance of the Hidalgo stachys leaves. This is a sensual pleasure that gardeners too rarely exploit. It is used to its fullest here.

There are microclimates within this microclimate. Plants that benefit from shade in wintertime, for example, are tucked in against the southern wall of the old foundation where the low winter sun will not reach them, and plants that need winter heat are set at the sun-drenched foot of the north wall.

In the end, it is all a matter of making skillful use of what the site provides. The challenge for the gardener lies in recognizing the potentials. You have to really look and analyze every feature. You have to, as Louis Bauer puts it, "look and feel like a plant."

BELOW

Thanks to nearly perfect drainage and its south-facing site, the Dry Garden overwinters many species formerly considered not hardy in New York.

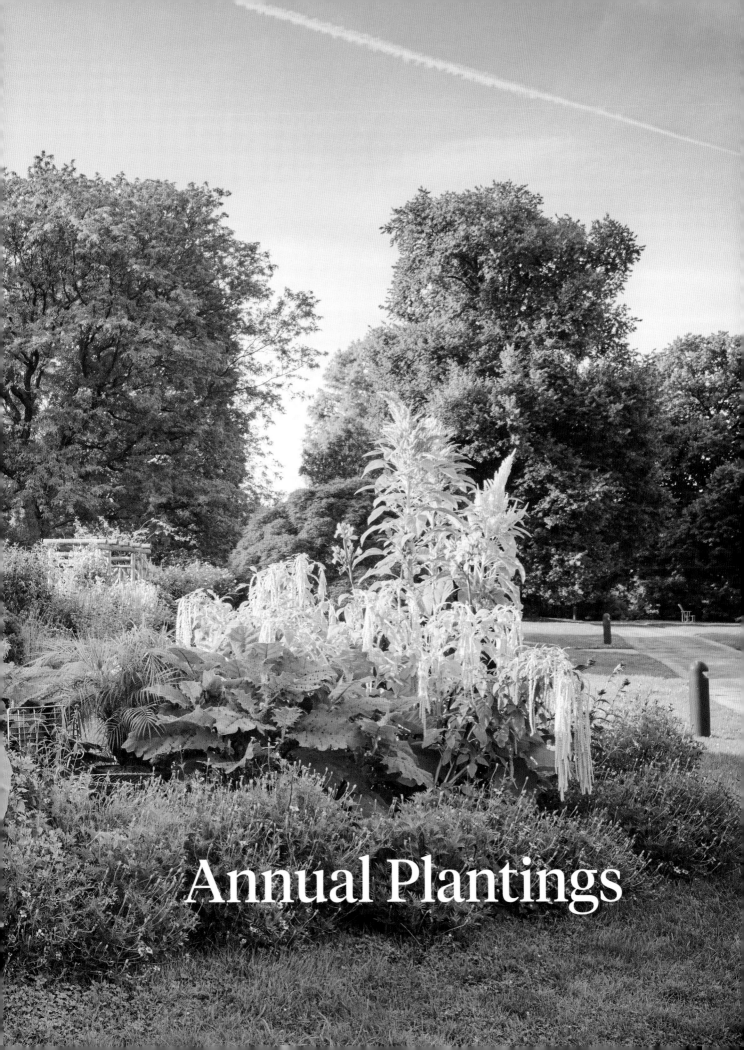

Annual Plantings

The bed itself was an inheritance from the old days, from when Wave Hill had been a private estate. In truth, it wasn't a particularly inspiring legacy. Set just to the west of the ruins of the glasshouses (the site of the future Marco Polo Stufano Conservatory), the bed was shaped like a curved teardrop approximately 36 feet long and 12 feet across at its widest point. The new Wave Hill staff named it the Paisley Bed because of its resemblance to that classic decorative motif.

When Marco Polo Stufano arrived on the scene at Wave Hill, this bed was planted entirely with dwarf deutzias, deciduous shrubs covered with small, bell-shaped, fragrant white flowers for a couple of weeks in spring. For the rest of the growing season, though, the Paisley Bed was just a patch of green. Most probably, this unimaginative planting was a legacy of the brief period when Wave Hill had been managed by the New York City Parks Department. In any event, change was overdue.

Accordingly, one spring early in Stufano's tenure, Wave Hill's new gardeners grubbed out the shrubbery and installed a colorful, if somewhat obvious, display of annual flowers: silver dusty miller (*Jacobaea maritima*) and scarlet zonal geraniums (*Pelargonium ×hortorum*). This was a predictable planting in its own way, one that was duplicated in public parks all over the United States. Stufano is embarrassed to recall it now. Even at the time, he knew that Wave Hill could do better.

Collectively, the staff turned its imagination loose and redefined the concept of "annual." Technically, of course, an annual flower is one that sprouts from seed, grows, flowers, and then dies, all within a single growing season. But broadening the category to include any plant that could be brought to maturity and flowering in a single season opened up new vistas. Many plants that are perennial in their native habitats but

can't withstand the New York winters could be grown as annuals. Some such transplants were, the gardeners realized, outstandingly adapted to a Bronx summer, with its virtually tropical heat and humidity.

The staff had the benefit of a historical perspective, thanks to Stufano's reading during his days as a student at the New York Botanical Garden. He was familiar with Victorian gardening literature, in particular the books of Andrew Jackson Downing, the first American landscape architect of note and a mentor to the designers of New York's Central Park. In such books as *Cottage Residences: Or, a Series of Designs for Rural Cottages and Cottage Villas, and Their Gardens and Grounds, Adapted to North America* (1853), Downing promoted the use of "exotics," plants just then coming into American horticulture from newly explored, frequently tropical, regions of the world. Although such plants, Downing noted, must be overwintered in the protection of a glasshouse or pit house, they "bloom and grow from May to November in the open flower garden." Using verbenas and scarlet geraniums as examples, he extolled "their many varieties, their brilliant colors, and their power of withstanding heat and dry weather." He asserted they had done more to give an air of perpetual beauty to flower gardens "than all other plants together." In another work, *A Treatise on the Theory and Practice of Landscape Gardening* (1859), Downing showed not only many plans involving curvilinear flower beds remarkably similar to the Paisley Bed, he also included an engraving of a view of his own Hudson Valley home, which was fronted by palms and a yucca in tubs.

Why not include such lush exotics in the planting of this latter-day Hudson River estate? The definition of what could go into the Paisley Bed expanded further.

What ensued was increasingly imaginative and unpredictable, something that had not been seen before in American annual plantings, and perhaps not anywhere else. Every year was different. The spring would start off with the bed packed with spring bulbs, pre-eminently collections of tulips chosen for their contrasting shades and heights. Then, when the spring bulbs had passed, they would be uprooted and the redefined annuals would be planted. One year, everything might be red, another year it might be a blaze of orange and yellow. In this bed, Wave Hill began an exploration of aesthetic frontiers.

While their impermanence is commonly seen as annual plants' main drawback, the fact that they don't persist more than one growing season becomes an advantage for the experimentalist. If the design scheme for a perennial planting doesn't work out, the gardener has lost a considerable investment: money spent at nurseries for plants and several years of nurturing before the perennials mature. Who wants to risk all that?

With annuals, especially if you grow them from seed or cuttings as Wave Hill typically does, the investment in dollars is slight, as is the time—a single growing season. If a daring plan works out, you have a triumph. If it doesn't, well, you were going to remove it come fall anyway.

The annual plantings did become increasingly daring, or at least unconventional. One summer that stands out in the memory of both Louis Bauer and Stufano followed a disastrous fire in the garage where they overwintered many semi-hardy plants. In picking through the wreckage to rescue the plants that had survived the conflagration, Stufano noticed that the long strips of copper flashing from the building's roof had, thanks to the intense heat, taken on a spectacular iridescence of related colors. Twisting the strips into an artful tangle, Marco set them out in the Paisley Bed as a sculptural element, then surrounded and intermingled them with annuals whose flower and foliage colors echoed those of the copper. He even managed to include some of the plant survivors from the ruined garage, turning the Paisley Bed into a sort of botanical phoenix, at least for that year.

The size of the Paisley Bed is crucial to its impact. Big enough to make a splash, it's still small enough that visitors can imagine translating its schemes to their own properties. Indeed, one year Bauer made an explicit play for that. Dividing the Paisley Bed in half with a picket fence and gate, he planted one half as a front yard with a colorful, cottage-style

A spring planting of tulips, underplanted with viola 'Sorbet Morpho' and 'Sorbet Midnight Glow'. Purple and yellow in a complementary contrast: annuals invite such daring color schemes.

tangle of flowers, and the other half, the backyard, with decorative rows of lush lettuces and other colorful annual vegetables.

Leafy vegetables are also elements on which Shane Pritchett, the gardener in charge of the Kate French Terrace, draws. The Terrace sits on the western edge of Wave Hill House, an historic English-style country manor house. His responsibilities here include a number of beds bracketing a rectangle of gray flagstones, with tables and chairs adjoining The Café at Wave Hill. Here, too, there is a spring and a summer display. But the fact is that throughout the growing season, with a brief pause when the bulbs are swapped for plants in late spring, this area must always look good.

Because visitors sit on the terrace to enjoy a cup of coffee or a meal, it makes an outsized contribution to the picture of the gardens that visitors take home. The terrace plantings have to look good well into September, as this area hosts cocktails and hors d'oeuvres during the Gardeners' Party, Wave Hill's annual fall fundraiser.

The tropical plants included with the annuals in these beds play a special role, because they have greater stamina. The true annuals are genetically programmed to die once they set seed. Even if the flowers are pinched off as they wither, before they can actually produce seeds, the annuals tend to exhaust themselves midway into the growing season. In many cases they can be revitalized by being cut back, to stimulate new growth, but that creates an interval of unattractiveness. The tropical plants, by contrast, most of which are perennials in their native ranges, just get bigger, bolder, and better as the season advances.

Pritchett has become adept at playing to the different seasons. Recently, he included in the spring display not only bulbs, such as the purple-leaved tulip 'Juan' and the white-flowered garlic (*Allium nigrum*), but also such

OPPOSITE

Using common plants in an uncommon fashion can expose new beauties. Here, French marigolds (*Tagetes patula*) positively glow when silhouetted against a pale chartreuse taro (*Colocasia esculenta* 'Maui Gold').

BELOW

Strong contrasts lend drama to a planting—love-lies-bleeding (*Amaranthus caudatus* 'Green Cascade') at top and center invites a stroking hand, while the naranjillo (*Solanum quitoense*) below warns off admirers with its spiked leaves.

The strongly architectural setting of the terrace encourages a more formal style of planting.

ABOVE RIGHT

A small tree fern (*Blechnum brasiliense*), surrounded by tropical foliage in a bright red-and-gold scheme.

OPPOSITE

The power of opposites: flamboyant tropical plantings erupt from the formal terrace in the boldest of contrasts, with black *Colocasia* 'Diamond Head' in a former fountain.

unconventional foliage plants as the red-leaved deer tongue lettuce 'Really Red Deer Tongue' and the chartreuse-leaved mustard 'Golden Streaks'. Backing these up were a number of annuals that naturally flourish during the cool weather of spring. These included not only the traditional choice of violas, such as the early-flowering 'Sorbet Orchid Rose Beacon', but also such unconventional selections as the so-called woodland tidytips (*Layia gaillardioides*) from the California coastal range and the poor man's orchid (*Schizanthus pinnatus*) from the mountains of Chile.

Annual Plantings

Such high-performance plantings demand high-performance soils. The Paisley Bed is amended twice a year, with wheelbarrow loads of compost dug in before each time it is planted. The result is a medium so organically rich and moisture-retentive that it never requires fertilization and rarely needs irrigation, other than what it picks up from the watering of the surrounding lawn during the heat of the summer. In fact, the soil is too rich for some plants to grow well, such as succulents that prefer a leaner mix. In general, though, annuals and tropicals grown as annuals, both of which have only a relatively short window in which to grow and bloom, need the resources they can extract from such a soil.

Something similar takes place in the Kate French Terrace beds. The constant infusion of potting soil that is added with the root balls of transplants grown in the glasshouses is sufficient to maintain a high organic level. Here, though, fertilization is necessary: a liquid fertilizer relatively rich in nitrogen—an NPK formula of 9-3-6—is mixed with water and applied a couple of times each summer.

ANNUALS IN CONTAINERS

An essential element of all annual displays at Wave Hill, container plantings reinforce the in-ground plantings in many ways. They serve as visual focal points and punctuation marks that, when repeated through-out a display, create a powerful rhythm. By extending plantings from the beds onto adjacent pavements, they provide not only an opportunity for additional planting even on impervious surfaces, they also blur and soften the line dividing hardscape from greenscape, helping to unify the landscape into a collective whole.

On the Kate French Terrace, many of the containers are memorable in their own right. A strawberry pot planted with lettuce, for example, creates a column of red leaves while also putting a new twist on an old tradition. However, rather than treating containers as freestanding individuals, with the conventional "thriller, filler, spiller" planting, the pots here are clustered together, coordinated in a quilt rather than treated as an assemblage of competing individuals.

Each pot in one of these clusters generally hosts a single type of plant. This simplifies maintenance—all the individual plants in a pot can be watered and fertilized according to the same schedule—and it also emboldens the contrasts. A whole pot of some fine-textured, silver foliage makes a stronger statement than just one specimen, especially when posed against another pot full of some scarlet flower or red-leaved plant.

Contrast is at the heart of an effective container grouping. Contrasts of flower colors, of course, but also of foliage textures and leaf shapes and sizes. The various elements of each grouping must have elements of similarity that link them one to another, but also strong dissimilarities to create drama.

The final designing is always done by eye on the spot. The Wave Hill gardeners testify that they never know exactly how a grouping will look until they are actually arranging the pots.

Rather than treating each container as an independent statement, the Wave Hill gardeners use pots as pieces of a greater whole.

Surely the greatest design challenge for any of Wave Hill's annual plantings is that of the Pergola, which is managed by gardener Jen Cimino. This collection of planters and beds has an overwhelming setting—it was built to frame a panoramic view of the Hudson River and the high, stone Palisades, the cliffs on the river's opposite, western shore. To try to compete with this would be fatal. Working with the view is the key.

This does not minimize the importance of the annual plantings around the foot of the Pergola. Rather, they become a crucial means to integrate the landscape's foreground and background. Autumn is the time when the view is most spectacular, as the leaves of trees along the Palisades take on their fall colors. Cimino makes sure to include those hues in her border. In a recent incarnation of this area, for instance, when the dominant theme was a contrast of white flowers and black foliages, she slipped in a licorice weed (*Scoparia dulcis* 'Illumina Lemon Mist') with

yellow, star-shaped flowers, two types of bloodleaf (*Iresine*), and coleus (*Plectranthus* 'Kiwi Fern') that flaunt a palette of autumn colors—red, purple, and yellow—in its frilly foliage.

This echoing of distant colors recalls a classic Japanese gardening technique called *shakkei*, which translates as "borrowed scenery." Essentially, the view is framed, as by Wave Hill's Pergola, to focus on some particularly attractive distant feature—in this case, the natural stone ramparts of the Hudson River Palisades with their forested top. Then some feature or features are included in the foreground of the garden to link the nearby landscape to the distant one, making the view a part of the garden. Here, the link is the mimicking of the colors of the

OPPOSITE

The Pergola plantings create a frame and a foreground to heighten the effect of the view. Here, pots of *Bellis perennis* have been added to the regularly changing group.

BELOW LEFT

As well as displaying beds and containers, the Pergola creates an opportunity to showcase hanging plants.

BELOW

Reddish orange notes in these containers will "borrow scenery" when the autumnal foliage comes to the Palisades.

LEFT TO RIGHT

A canopy of hardy kiwi (*Actinidia arguta*) completes the Pergola's living frame of the panoramic view.

A walkway under the Pergola provides views of the Hudson and Palisades.

The solidity of its architectural niches only emphasizes the delicacy of this hybrid begonia (*Begonia* 'Starry Nights').

autumn foliage atop the Palisades by plants within the garden. The impression of continuity expands the borders of the garden, integrating the view into the composition. In this way, Wave Hill's Pergola becomes a portal to the drama of the magnificent distant cliffs.

Inspiration for these annual displays comes from many sources: ideas or plant combinations observed during visits to other gardens, or color associations taken from artworks. One theme idea even came from the news: in 2017, the Paisley Bed featured plants from seven, mostly Islamic, countries that were targeted in a Federal travel ban.

On the terrace, Shane Pritchett assembles spreadsheets featuring photographs of annuals that have caught his eye. On the Pergola, Jen Cimino recently began working from a dream she had of a silver and orange border. She's going to make that dream a reality. You can do that with annuals.

Pergola with fall foliage. Between the columns, the Palisades can be seen across the river, reflecting the autumn sun.

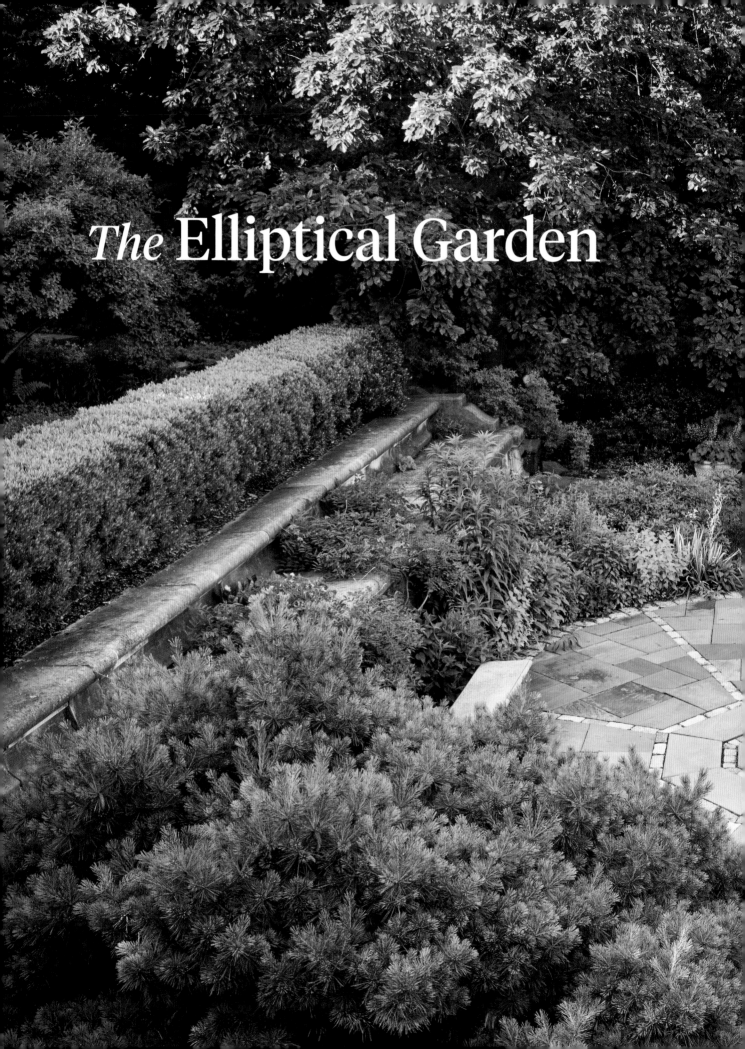

The Elliptical Garden

PREVIOUS SPREAD

A view of the Elliptical Garden from the
north.

OPPOSITE

The entrance to the Elliptical Garden,
Wave Hill's display of native plants.
Skullcap (*Scutellaria galericulata*) and
purple-flowering raspberry (*Rubus
odoratus*) bloom along the path.

BELOW

To demonstrate the potential of natives
in the home landscape, Wave Hill chose
to plant them in a formal setting. In this
June scene, coral bells (*Heuchera* 'Mocha')
bloom in the urn, bowman's root (*Gillenia
trifoliata*) blooms at right.

There are two ways to interpret Wave Hill's relationship to native
plants. From the perspective of purists, those who in recent
years have come to insist that only native plants should be used in the
garden, Wave Hill is out of step. But spend an afternoon in the Elliptical
Garden and another interpretation becomes
more persuasive. It seems in the matter of native
plants, as has so often been the case, Wave Hill
may simply be a step ahead of the trends.

It's true that the gardeners here rarely factor
country of origin into their decisions about
whether to include a plant in the landscapes.
For the most part, Wave Hill is cheerfully
cosmopolitan. North American natives are often
included in plantings, but only if they add to a
display in terms of texture, color, or structure.
In addition, they must be able to coexist with
plants from every other continent (except, of
course, ice-bound Antarctica).

There is one area of Wave Hill, however, where
provenance is crucial. That is the Elliptical
Garden, where the flora is all native to eastern
North America. Typically, though, Wave Hill has
used these by-now familiar ingredients in an
innovative and unexpected way.

Marco Polo Stufano had worked in the NYBG's
Native Plants Garden when he was a student
there in the mid-1960s. So he was well aware

May in the Elliptical Garden: moss phlox (*Phlox subulata*) in full bloom with *Heuchera* 'Caramel' for contrast.

of the fascination these plants can stir, and of their distinctive beauty. By the mid-1990s, what had been an interest of a few botanically minded *cognoscenti* was becoming a powerful and popular movement. As gardens based on native flora became more common, Stufano decided that Wave Hill should have such a feature, too. But whereas virtually every other native-plants garden (including the one at the New York Botanical Garden) was naturalistic in design, an attempt to assemble the various plants into some counterfeit of a natural habitat, the one at Wave Hill was to be of a formal design.

This didn't just spring from some contrarian impulse. Stufano had noticed the reluctance that many homeowners had to converting their domestic landscapes into a simulation of the wilderness. If natives were to become as widely planted as their supporters hoped, alternatives had to be offered that would suit a variety of tastes. A more domesticated alternative was what Wave Hill set out to create.

The site selected for this project was at the edge of Wave Hill's own natural area, the eight acres of the Herbert and Hyonja Abrons Woodland that girdle the gardens and houses. Specifically, it was the site of a disused swimming pool, yet another relic from Wave Hill's past as a family home. The pool had been drained and filled in. Rectangular in shape, it was set into a niche carved from a terrace overlooking the slope down to the Hudson River. The pool was paved over with bluestone, and became the centerpiece for a quartet of symmetrical, neatly delineated beds.

What this area shares with the rest of Wave Hill's gardens is a meticulous style of planting. The space was first carefully structured with shrubs and compact trees. Hedges of inkberry holly (*Ilex glabra*) and American holly (*Ilex opaca*) edge and define the space. Eastern red cedars (*Juniperus virginiana*) mark two of the corners, and a pair of dwarf white pines (*Pinus strobus* 'Nana') flank the entrance to the adjacent Ecology Building.

Gardening with Natives from Seed

Availability of native plants has improved over the last decade so that selections are now found at many local nurseries, garden centers, and even big-box stores. For a broader assortment, the gardener can turn to mail-order suppliers. But for the real rarities, fanciers may still have to start their own plants from seed, as Wave Hill does.

There are a number of benefits to starting plants from seed. Economy is certainly one of them, as seeds cost a fraction of nursery-grown plants. Wave Hill's gardeners stretch their budgets this way. Another advantage is the broader selection of species and cultivars available to this sort of horticultural do-it-yourselfer. In particular, plant societies such as the North American Rock Garden Society make a wealth of flora available to members through seed exchanges, including many natives obtainable nowhere else.

Yet another benefit, and perhaps the most important, is the intimate knowledge of a plant that derives from the process of starting it from seed. Virtually every plant has some mechanism for delaying the germination of the seed so that it doesn't sprout while still on the plant or during inappropriate seasons of the year. In most cases, these mechanisms reflect the habitat and circumstances in which the plant naturally occurs. The seeds of an annual plant native to northern regions, for example, may need a period of chilling before they germinate. This ensures that the seeds remain dormant until winter has passed, so that they don't start growing until the more benevolent weather of spring arrives.

Other factors that can enforce dormancy include a hard coating that must age and crack before the seed inside can germinate, a need for a period of moisture and warmth, repeated soakings, or even alternating periods of cold and warmth. Knowing the climate and conditions to which the plant is accustomed can explain and suggest which conditions must be satisfied to coax its seeds out of dormancy. At the same time, the factors governing seed dormancy also suggest what sort of conditions are characteristic of that plant's habitat.

Wave Hill's gardeners use a variety of handbooks and other resources to determine what conditions must be satisfied to awaken a given type of seed from dormancy. For the home gardener, the information included on seed packets and in better catalogs is usually sufficient. For additional information, the gardener can refer to an excellent guide to starting seeds of native North American plants published by the Wild Ones, an organization with many local chapters that promotes natural landscaping with native plants. The manual *Germination Instructions for Seeds* is available without cost online at wildones.org/wp-content/uploads/2012/09/004cGerminationInstructionsFinalRevision.pdf.

For the advanced seed-starter, there is the more scientific manual that the Wave Hill gardeners use, *Seed Germination Theory and Practice*, self-published by the author, Norman C. Deno, a professor emeritus of chemistry at Pennsylvania State University. This volume explores the chemical and physical mechanisms that cause dormancy, with detailed instructions on how to overcome each of them. Most valuable is the extensive, alphabetically arranged list of plant genera at the end of the book, with advice on how to overcome the dormancy (if any) of the respective seeds.

Around these woody plants are disposed masses of native perennials, all selected to provide contrast and harmonies of texture and color, as well as a season-long display of flowers. No effort has been made to reproduce a particular community of plants. Rather, this is a more conventional, albeit highly artful, display in which species from disparate habitats are combined to create a succession of exciting compositions from spring through fall. The point is well made here that natives can serve as elements of a sophisticated garden picture, that they need not be confined to artificial reconstructions of natural habitats.

There are many lessons to be learned here. For example, there is the vine patterning the wall on the eastern, uphill, side of the garden, a precisely espaliered American wisteria (*Wisteria macrostachya* 'Blue Moon'). This espalier gives the lie to one of the most common criticisms of native plants, that because they come straight from the wild they tend to be unruly. Unlike its better-known Asian relatives, the American wisteria does not send up suckers from its roots and so is much easier to control in the garden. Although vigorous, it is not rampant like the Chinese (*W. sinensis*) and Japanese (*W. floribunda*) wisterias and is easily contained by pruning. The Wave Hill specimen demonstrates how attractive a native wisteria can be.

Experience at Wave Hill indicates that natives are no more intrinsically unruly than any other class of plants. But neither have they proven, as their fans like to claim, more self-sufficient, at least not in the garden. When chosen to fit the characteristics of the site and the local climate, they generally thrive—true, of course, of any plants.

One respect in which native plants differ from those introduced from abroad is in their relationship to local insect populations. Not so long ago, it was often argued that because native plants had co-evolved with

Along this path, a clipped hedge of inkberry holly (*Ilex glabra* 'Shamrock'); at left, pink-flowered moss phlox and blue cultivars of woodland phlox (*Phlox divaricata*).

OPPOSITE

Moss phlox (*Phlox subulata* 'Emerald Cushion Blue').

Kentucky wisteria (*Wisteria macrostachya* 'Blue Moon') espaliered against a wall shows how mannerly natives can be.

these pests they had somehow developed a resistance to them. That may be true in individual instances, but in general, because they are familiar, the plants indigenous to a region are actually more likely to be targeted by the local herbivorous insects.

Consider the comparison that Douglas W. Tallamy, a professor of entomology and wildlife ecology at the University of Delaware, made between a young native white oak (*Quercus alba*) in his own yard and the Asian-descended Bradford pear (*Pyrus calleryana* 'Bradford') in his neighbor's garden. Although both trees were approximately the same size, Tallamy found 410 caterpillars of 19 species on the oak and only one individual caterpillar on the foreign pear. Repeating his count the following day with another white oak and pear, he found 233 caterpillars of 15 species on the former and again just one individual on the latter.

There are two potential responses to this finding. Gardeners who want a garden free of insect damage and who don't espouse pesticides may deliberately opt for the native-insect-resistant exotic plants. Those, however, who don't mind a certain amount of herbivory may choose to support food sources for birds and other wildlife.

LEFT TO RIGHT

'Blue Moon' Kentucky wisteria in full bloom.

False indigo (*Baptisia* 'Purple Smoke') provides a backdrop for a garden rest stop.

Bowman's root (*Porteranthus trifoliatus*) in June.

Just maybe that choice, and the knowledge it entails, speaks to the true value of native plants. They let the gardener experience nature in full. And that may be the best reason to include them in your garden—whether formal or informal.

OPPOSITE, CLOCKWISE FROM TOP LEFT

Prairie natives such as Joe Pye weed (*Eutrochium maculatum*), coneflower (*Echinacea* cultivars), and yellow-flowered annual partridge pea (*Chamaecrista fasciculata*) contribute bloom to the Elliptical Garden in midsummer; partridge pea reseeds freely in the Elliptical Garden; statuesque swamp sunflower (*Helianthus angustifolius* 'Matanzas Creek') blooms in fall, extending the Elliptical Garden's display until frost; like most prairie plants, brown-eyed Susan (*Rudbeckia triloba*) is a summer bloomer.

BELOW LEFT

Blue cardinal flower (*Lobelia siphilitica*) and Joe Pye weed (*Eutrochium maculatum*), seen here blooming in midsummer, naturally inhabit wet ground but tolerate ordinary garden soil if it is kept consistently moist.

BELOW

Purple blossoms of New York ironweed (*Vernonia noveboracensis*) complement the clear blue of great blue lobelia (*Lobelia siphilitica*).

The Elliptical Garden

The Conservatory

PREVIOUS SPREAD

The Marco Polo Stufano Conservatory,
Wave Hill's wintertime retreat.

OPPOSITE

Plants in terra-cotta pots echo the
terra-cotta tile floor of the Palm House.

The goal of a skilled garden designer is to create a true twelve-month experience, a landscape that is interesting and rewarding any time of year. This is challenging in the temperate parts of North America, where the gardener must cope with a period of winter dormancy. Wave Hill confronts this challenge in a number of ways. Even when the plants are dormant, there are the ever-changing views of the Hudson River and its western shore, all skillfully presented in calculated vistas. Wintertime strips the gardens of flowers and much of its foliage, but that subtraction brings into high relief the carefully conceived structure underneath, the forms of the naked trees and shrubs, the bulk of the evergreens, the rocks, paths, pergolas, and gazebos that punctuate and form the space. And when cold weather proves too much, there is always the refuge of the Marco Polo Stufano Conservatory.

To be fair, this is not just a wintertime escape; much of the conservatory remains well worth a visit year-round. But it is when the cold outdoors is intense that the habitats inside the glass walls and roofs are most seductive.

Slipping through the Beaux Arts entrance to the conservatory's Palm House, the central portion of the building, one is met with a waft of warm, humid air, heavy with the fecund odor peculiar to glasshouses. Exotic and evergreen vines, shrubs, and trees—Cape leadwort (*Plumbago auriculata*), silver dollar tree (*Eucalyptus cinerea*), flame vine (*Pyrostegia venusta*), *Bougainvillea* 'Firecracker Red', white Lady Banks rose (*Rosa banksiae* 'Alba-Plena'), and the purple form of Cootamundra wattle (*Acacia baileyana* var. *purpurea*)—cover the walls, bearing extravagant, perfumed blossoms. Groupings of pots ornament the terra-cotta tile floor, offering clusters of flowers and foliage as carefully arranged as any floral designer's bouquet. Like a floral arrangement, too, the

A yellow-flowered acacia (*Acacia baileyana*) stands sentinel by the door leading from the Palm House to the Tropical House. Blue-flowered desertbells (*Phacelia campanularia*) and the white sprays of iboza (*Tetradenia riparia*) bloom to the front and left.

ABOVE RIGHT

Like sunshine in midwinter, the flowers of *Acacia baileyana* brighten the Palm House.

disposition of the pots in the Palm House changes constantly, with new pots brought in from the other parts of the conservatory and even from a plastic-covered hoop house nearby, as plants come into bloom. There are visitors who come every week in the winter and early spring to savor the changes, the additions, and the subtractions.

To the right, up a flight of stairs at the east end of the Palm House, is the drier setting of the Cactus and Succulent House, with its more disciplined ranks of fleshy, spiked specimens. Laid out on waist-high display tables (or benches) are cacti, natives only of the New World. Opposite are similar benches covered with the succulent plants of the Old World. Despite the occasional flower, this is primarily a display of architecture. The succulent pattern of growth is a response to a dry, sunny, desiccating environment, with the parts of the plant reduced to the most compact forms with the least surface area—spheres, pleated columns, sunbursts of fat leaves, and skeletons in which leaves have been transformed into spines and twigs into linear reservoirs. With 400 to 500 specimens, this house provides a fair encyclopedia of how drought conditions can change plants.

The western end of the Palm House leads, through a glass door, to the Tropical House. This is maintained at a high humidity: in addition to the water administered to the plants, the floor and radiators are wet with the hose three times a day. The roof as well is coated with a light-reflective paint during sunnier seasons, and the overall goal is to create a jungle understory of filtered light that is packed with ferns, bromeliads that harvest their moisture from the air, and other tender plants. The flavor of their native habitat is preserved in the way that many of these tropical

Two images of the Cactus and Succulent House: New World cacti to the left, and Old World succulents on the right.

natives are displayed: epiphytic bromeliads mounted on a log, or ferns hung suspended as they might be in a jungle tree.

Finally, although the public is not invited into this area, adjacent to the conservatory is a house devoted to propagating the plants that Wave Hill uses in Palm House displays and in its outdoor gardens. More utilitarian in aspect, the Propagation House hosts the seedlings and cuttings in orderly rows on benches topped with crushed stone.

Constructed in 1969, the Marco Polo Stufano Conservatory is not the first assemblage of glasshouses on this site. In fact, it follows exactly the footprint of glasshouses built during Wave Hill's years as a private estate. Those old glasshouses fell derelict after the city took ownership of the property and before Marco Polo Stufano's arrival, and had to be pulled down. The grand entrance to the Palm House was preserved and incorporated into the new, modernistic structure, to retain a taste of what was there before.

The goal in rebuilding the glasshouses was partly to preserve Wave Hill's heritage as a private estate. In addition, these structures provide a focal point for the surrounding gardens, a visual pivot around which they revolve. The glasshouses are also a center of interest, playing a crucial role in the functioning of the gardens. The plants they support are, one might say, seasonal commuters, because once the weather warms, these hothouse subjects migrate outside. They supply a reservoir of foliage, form, and color on which the gardeners draw to add extra substance to beds, borders, and containers throughout the landscape. Most are chosen in part for their ability to perform this double duty, indoors and out.

The cacti and Old World succulents in the Cactus and Succulent House, for example, with their dramatic, architectural forms, make natural garden ornaments. A large agave, with its spiky rosette, is a piece of living sculpture, a natural centerpiece around which to arrange a collection of potted plants. A barrel cactus is perfectly at home making a spiny statement in the heat and drought of a sun-drenched, stone-paved terrace.

The Tropical House, by contrast, supports a host of cuttings of coleus (*Plectranthus scutellarioides*), spurflowers (*Plectranthus* species),

OPPOSITE

Hung with bromeliads and other tree-dwelling plants, the Tropical House mimics the conditions of the jungle understory.

OPPOSITE

Spider iris (*Ferraria crispa*), a native of the South African
rocks, thrives in the Palm House.

ABOVE

A *Coelogyne* orchid comes to the Palm House from
Southeast Asia.

ornamental sweet potatoes (*Ipomoea batatas*) to flesh out containers and beds, as well as such flashy foliar punctuations as the 'Truly Tiny' compact banana.

Flora for the Palm House includes many southern-hemisphere plants that flourish and bloom in late winter or early spring, and for the most part they summer outdoors in a maintenance area closed to the public—they are not at their best in the hot weather. Yet the Palm House also includes many, many specimens that make contributions to the summertime gardens. Laurustinus (*Viburnum tinus*), an evergreen shrub marginally hardy in Wave Hill's USDA zone 7, bears fragrant white blossoms indoors in winter and early spring, but flaunts clusters of metallic blue berries outdoors in the summer and often into fall, when it is returned to the conservatory.

Each type of plant in the various houses within the conservatory demands its own customized care, but there are some generalities. Unglazed clay pots are used for all the plants except the handful that are rooted right into pockets of soil in the Palm House floor. The cost of clay pots is much greater than that of plastic equivalents, but the gardeners at Wave Hill have found that the superior environment provided by clay is worth the expense. The porosity of clay allows air and moisture to penetrate the sides of the pot. This moisture and air are used by the fine roots located at the edge of the soil ball inside the pot. Clay pots also act like a wick to remove excess moisture from the potting soil, helping protect the plants inside them from overwatering. For the same reason, plants grown in clay pots typically require more frequent irrigation. In particular, plants which require a well-drained, dryish soil, such as cacti and succulents, grow better when potted into clay. When the temperature in the glasshouses rises, the water passing out through the clay and evaporating off the surface helps to keep the pots cool, protecting roots against overheating.

OPPOSITE, CLOCKWISE FROM TOP LEFT

Purple bell vine (*Rhodochiton atrosanguineus*) from Mexico twines around its support.

A gladiolus (*Gladiolus tristis* var. *concolor*) vies for position with a South African sand lily (*Veltheimia capensis* var. *rosea*).

A January blossom on *Camellia japonica* 'Tinsie' (syn. *C. japonica* 'Bokuhan').

Natal lily (*Clivia miniata*), native to South Africa and Swaziland, blooms from December to April.

BELOW

A display of tree-dwelling (epiphytic) bromeliads in the Tropical House.

Potting Mix

The foundation of healthy indoor plants lies in the potting mixture. The rate at which it drains, its fertility, texture, and organic content determine whether the plant's roots flourish, and this in turn determines the health of the plant overall. Different types of plants require different potting mixes; Wave Hill uses about 15 different potting mixes. The recipe shared below is for Wave Hill's general purpose mix #11—the mix used for most perennials, annuals, and the general run of tropicals.

Each part = 1 bucket (approx. 2 gallons)
Each scoop = approx. 1 quart

General Mix #11

Vermiculite	2 parts
Perlite	5 parts
Peat moss	6 parts
Loam or topsoil	4 parts
Sand	2 parts
Charcoal	1 part
Bonemeal	2 scoops
Limestone	1 cup

Mix contents thoroughly and then pasteurize (heat) the potting soil to a temperature sufficient to kill pathogens (disease-causing fungi and bacteria), insects, and weed seeds without killing beneficial soil organisms. In the home, pasteurization is best done by filling a large roasting pan with moistened (but not wet) potting soil and covering it with foil. Put the roaster full of soil into a 200–250°F oven and monitor the soil temperature with a food thermometer. When the thermometer shows the potting mix has reached an interior temperature of 140°F, start timing. After 30 minutes at 140°F, the potting soil is ready to be removed from the oven. Do not overheat the potting mix as that can damage soil structure, kill beneficial soil organisms, and even release plant toxins.

OPPOSITE, CLOCKWISE FROM TOP LEFT

Ornamental leaves with red markings add extra color to *Monolena primuliflora*, an epiphyte from Ecuador and Peru.

Clerodendrum (*Clerodendrum incisum*) dangles buds that resemble the notes of a scale.

Called flowering maple because of its large, dissected, evergreen leaves, *Abutilon* 'Clementine' bears large red blossoms.

Relatives of the African violet, kohlerias (*Kohleria* species) were a Victorian favorite. This hybrid, *K.* 'Rebecka', thrives in Wave Hill's Tropical House.

The Wave Hill gardeners are also agreed on a philosophy of growing the plants lean. Pumping the plants up with more fertilizer than is needed results in soft, overly lush growth that is not only unattractive but also highly prone to pests, especially aphids. Instead, the conservatory gardeners take care to fertilize only when the plants are actively growing—the Old World succulents, for example, mostly originated in South Africa and Madagascar and they go dormant during periods of high heat, making most of their new growth in late winter and early spring. The New World succulents experience colder winters and often don't start their principal growth until late April or May. The southern hemisphere plants of the Palm House also go dormant during the summer and are moved outside. In their native habitat, their period of growth comes during the moister, cooler winter, and so at Wave Hill they are fed during the winter, not the summer.

In any case, the fertilization is typically sparing: gardeners in the glasshouses use water-soluble products that are mixed with irrigation water at the lowest recommended dosage. The frequency of these treatments varies with the vigor of the plant. Slow-growing succulents receive just four feedings a year, two during their spring growth and two more after the weather cools again in early fall. The tropicals, on the other hand, get weekly diluted feedings during the winter to fuel their more robust growth. Fertilizers are also varied to manipulate the growth of the plants. A high-nitrogen fertilizer, such as a 9-3-6 formula, for example, may be applied to encourage vigorous leaf growth, as with the tropical foliage plants, whereas a formula richer in phosphates (such as 3-12-6) is likely to be applied to enhance flowering of plants in the Palm House.

Irrigation varies with the needs of the plants for moisture, and so is markedly different from house to house. In the Cactus and Succulent House, it is typically sparing, the plants watered only when thoroughly dry. The Tropical House,

OPPOSITE

The Peruvian maidenhair fern (*Adiantum peruvianum*) sets off its large, flat pinnules with fine, ebony-colored stems.

BELOW

A rich diversity of form and architecture awaits the visitor to the Cactus and Succulent House.

on the other hand, is kept more moist to suit inhabitants that largely originated in rain forests and jungles. There, in addition to the measures taken to boost humidity, the watering is frequent, especially during hot weather. Again, though, irrigation is keyed to the plants' seasons of growth, because even tropicals will rot if they remain wet when not in active growth.

The different glasshouses are also kept at varying temperatures, to suit the flora inside. The Tropical House, for example, is maintained at a junglelike warmth, not less than 65–70°F and no more than 90°F. The Palm House, which houses mostly subtropical plants, is kept cooler, with a minimum temperature of 50°F. The hoop house adjacent to the conservatory is kept cooler yet, no more than 50°F, to suit the camellias, evergreen shrubs which, though frost-sensitive, require some winter chill.

With two estate houses located at opposite ends of the property—Wave Hill House to the north and Glyndor House to the south—the conservatory holds a central position within the gardens. But it is not the

OPPOSITE, CLOCKWISE FROM TOP LEFT

Specimens from the Cactus and Succulent House include *Aeonium arboreum* var. *atropurpureum* (top), *A.* 'Tricolor' (bottom left) and *A. lindleyi* var. *viscatum* (bottom center); silver hairs put the glint on the leaves of *Echeveria pulvinata* 'Frosty' in the New World section; a pair of euphorbias: *Euphorbia obesa* (front) and *E. horrida* 'Snowflake' (back); native to South Africa, *Haworthia cymbiformis* roots into rocky crevices subject to seasonal drought.

BELOW

Terra-cotta pots are the rule in Wave Hill's conservatory; here, they are neatly lined out on a bench in the Propagation House.

Starting seeds in the Propagation House. This facility greatly expands the flora accessible to the Wave Hill gardeners.

OPPOSITE

The conservatory's collections are a resource for the outdoor gardens in warmer seasons.

only collection of glasshouses accessible to the public in the Bronx. Its namesake Marco Polo Stufano describes Wave Hill's conservatory as "a minor melody" compared to the "symphony" of the grand crystal palace four miles away at the New York Botanical Garden. Stufano is convinced, however, that the more modest size of the Wave Hill indoor garden is, in some ways, an asset. People relate more easily to the smaller, more personal size of Wave Hill's conservatory, and they see the plants more clearly. In a bigger facility, individual plants merge into a botanical crowd and are, to a large extent, lost. In Wave Hill's conservatory, they remain specimens, carefully chosen and carefully displayed, to be savored one by one.

Living sculptures, these agaves center the Flower Garden in summertime.

Less grand than larger glasshouses, Wave Hill's Marco Polo Stufano Conservatory takes advantage of its more personal scale to display its plants as individual specimens, each worthy of note.

The Edges of Everything

PREVIOUS SPREAD

The Lower Lawn extends views of the
Hudson to another level, which is actually
the roof of Wave Hill's Ecology Building.

Attention to detail is an essential secret of fine craftsmanship, and nowhere is this more evident than in the gardens of Wave Hill. Choosing extraordinary plants is fundamental, as is the vision needed to arrange them so that they complement each other, melding into a single aesthetic statement. Yet the expression of these things is only as good as the actual execution of the plan. If the visitor encounters weeds, straggling plants, and poorly defined edges, then the first impression will be bad, and first impressions are notoriously hard to overcome. That is why Wave Hill's gardeners strive so hard to master and refine, as they put it, "the edges of everything."

This ethic dates back to the establishment of Wave Hill as a public space. It was central to the legacy handed down to Marco Polo Stufano by his teachers, the gardeners at the New York Botanical Garden. Especially influential was T.H. Everett, the British-trained director of horticulture at NYBG, who shared the craft he had learned as a gardener on private estates in England and as a student at the Royal Botanic Gardens, Kew. Details upon which Everett insisted in his work—the use of clay pots, the firming of soil into pots with fingertips rather than thumbs, of working bent over or squatting rather than sitting or kneeling on the ground— continue to be the rule at Wave Hill.

Jokingly referred to at Wave Hill as "the Queen's way" of doing things, these practices are not arbitrary but rather founded in a desire for excellence. Plants simply grow better in clay pots, if you are willing to support the extra expense. If you use your thumbs to firm down soil when potting or repotting plants, you tend to exert too much pressure, overcompressing the potting mix, which is why the use of fingertips is the rule. And although working bent over or stooped is uncomfortable

The Edges of Everything

The use of clay pots is an essential part of horticultural tradition at Wave Hill.

initially, it allows a gardener to better address the tasks of weeding or planting, and to work faster.

One hallmark of working at Wave Hill that has encouraged the creation of a body of institutional craft is the long tenure of the individual gardeners. Most, once they have hired on, stay for years, and many remain at Wave Hill for decades. These older gardeners, having learned the Wave Hill way of doing things, pass along resulting skills to new-comers. A number of the gardeners have been graduates of Wave Hill's horticultural internship program, so they have already been steeped in the garden's way of doing things before they sign on.

Getting Seeds Off to a Good Start

Although the seeds of various species may require different sorts of conditioning to coax them out of dormancy, in other respects, the treatment at Wave Hill follows a pattern.

- Seeds are sown into a peat-based, commercially available seed-starting mix, as this has antiseptic properties and helps protect against such diseases as damping-off that commonly attack seedlings. At Wave Hill, this is blended with ten percent coarse sand; a colorless aquarium gravel available at most pet stores works well.

- Three-inch-square pots are used to germinate the seeds. Into this is deposited first a layer one stone deep of three-eighths-inch gravel. Then the pot is filled with amended seed-starting mix, almost to the top. This is firmed into the pot and then the seed is scattered over its surface. If the recommendation is to cover the seed with more seed-starting mix, this is then sprinkled over the surface of the pot.

- The surface of the seed-starting mix is then dressed with a shallow layer of the same colorless aquarium gravel that was blended with the seed-starting mix. This surface coat protects the seeds from disturbance by water when the pot is irrigated or wet by rain.

- When the seeds have been sown and the sand applied, the surface of the contents of the pot should be level with the lip of the pot. By promoting the best possible air circulation around emerging seedlings, this reduces the risk of fungal diseases.

- A label is inserted into each pot to record the type of seed it contains and the date of sowing.

- Many seeds benefit from warmth when germinating; if this is the case, the pot, after watering, is set on a waterproof horticultural heating pad.

- Most of the seeds of cool, temperate plants need alternating periods of moist chilling and moist warmth. To furnish this, the seeds are sown in late summer or fall and then the pots are set outdoors in a bottomless wooden box covered with a lid of hardware cloth, to protect against squirrels and mice. The pots are left in this protective frame until their seeds have germinated and, usually, produced a pair of true leaves. (Seedlings typically emerge with just one or two cotyledons—simplified embryonic leaves—only subsequently bearing leaves of the more characteristic adult form.) When the seedlings reach this stage, they are pricked out. That is, the mass of seedlings is lifted out of the pot, teased apart, and replanted individually into small clay pots.

One of the more distinctive aspects of Wave Hill's gardening is its self-reliance: a remarkable proportion of the materials the staff uses are produced onsite. Especially important in this regard is the large heap tucked back in the woodland. It's where all the organic wastes, from plant trimmings to discarded annuals, are rotted down into compost and then used lavishly to condition and feed the soil. The preparation of annual beds in the Paisley Bed and the Pergola and on the Kate French Terrace involves using a garden fork to dig in four to six inches of compost every spring. Likewise, a couple of scoops of compost are added every time a new plant is inserted into the perennial beds in the Flower Garden and the Wild Garden.

Compost is added not just to enhance the structure of the soil, but also to enrich it. Even though compost, pound for pound, contains just a fraction of the nutrients found in chemical fertilizers, the staff prefers it because, unlike synthetic products, compost enhances the microflora and microfauna of the soil. In this way, it helps the soil to feed itself.

For similar reasons—including the health of the soil—overcultivation is avoided. Deep digging is undertaken only when a new bed is created or when, after many years, a bed requires a thorough renovation. The routine digging used in the yearly preparation of the annual beds extends down only one spit—one length of a spade's blade—deep.

A bed's preparation necessarily varies to suit the needs of the type of flora that will be planted there. For example, in 2015 when the beds were renovated in the Dry Garden, the soil was dug to a depth of two feet and mixed half and half with compost to ensure good drainage, then topped with a six-inch layer of fine gravel into which the plants were set. The Herb Garden beds, which were renovated at the same time, were dug to a similar depth and the soil in them mixed with compost and pasteurized loam. The goal in both

Thorough preparation of the soil—to enhance drainage and fertility—sets the stage for the lush growth of this lavender border.

cases was to create the conditions of fast drainage and modest fertility that plants in both the Dry Garden and Herb Garden prefer.

Such intensive soil preparation may seem onerous. In fact, though, because the quality of the soil determines the vigor of the plant's subsequent growth, skimping on the soil preparation is not a wise economy. The gardener will surely expend more time and effort nurturing a struggling plant than was saved by cutting corners before planting, and the results will be disappointing.

A full and verdant look is one of the signatures of Wave Hill gardening. Crucial to creating this is the well-timed pinch; the removal of a plant's growing tips at the proper stage encourages branching and thus denser, less lanky growth. In this way, pinching can reduce the need for staking.

Attending to details is about practicality as well as appearances. Here, an unmowable bank of sod was converted to a thriving border of *Hosta* 'Queen Josephine'.

Gardener Albert Cabrera pinches assiduously in the Gold Border so that he can largely eliminate the need for plant supports, whose look he does not like. Finally, because pinching also retards flowering, if applied to some portion of a drift of some perennial and not to the rest, it also lengthens the effective season of bloom by creating some stems that come into flower later than the rest.

Pinching is a technique used with many annuals, especially those grown for their foliage, such as coleus (*Plectranthus scutellarioides*), to create a bushier form. Among perennials, summer phlox (*Phlox paniculata*), sneezeweed (*Helenium autumnale* and hybrids), coneflowers (*Rudbeckia* species), asters (*Aster* and *Symphyotrichum* species), and hardy chrysanthemums (*Chrysanthemum* species and hybrids) are common targets for pinching. Plants that do not naturally branch but instead produce one terminal flower spike, like foxgloves (*Digitalis* species) and delphiniums (*Delphinium* species), are not good pinching candidates, nor are flowers which bloom from low rosettes, such as coral bells (*Heuchera* species), daylilies (*Hemerocallis*

The Edges of Everything

At the western end of the Shade Border, a Persian ironwood (*Parrotia persica*) tree overlooks a lush border of Hakone grass (*Hakonechloa macra*).

species), astilbes (*Astilbe* species), and irises (*Iris* species). In these cases, pinching back simply removes the flower buds.

Typically, the gardeners start the treatment toward the end of April, when the plants have developed six pairs of leaves. This first pinch removes half of a young shoot: the top three pairs of leaves. A lesser pinch, removing the topmost pair or two of leaves, may be imposed at two- to three-week intervals until the beginning of July, whereupon the plants are left to grow as they will.

Pinching or snipping with a sharp pair of shears is a technique also used to deadhead plants, that is, to remove the fading flowers before they can set seed. This is common practice; an unusual twist on this technique

is practiced at Wave Hill, however. The spring-blooming shrubs such as spireas (*Spiraea* species), neillias (*Neillia* species), forsythias (*Forsythia* ×*intermedia* hybrids), and mock oranges (*Philadelphus* species) that have colorful new growth or variegated foliage are deadheaded after they bloom, both to remove the unattractive seed heads but also to encourage a second flush of bright new leaves.

Staking and supporting plants are usually regarded as just tiresome tasks, but the gardeners at Wave Hill have raised the practice to the level of an art form. The supports are fashioned from natural fiber twines and mostly prunings collected on site; the results are not only effective but attractive. Though typically unobtrusive—the plants are the stars, after all—these handcrafted supports furnish a look of finish to the beds and borders.

The stems for the stakes are collected from the perennial plantings themselves, at the end of the growing season during fall cleanup, mostly from members of the pea family such as bush clovers (*Lespedeza* species) and false indigos (*Baptisia* species), supplemented with bamboo canes (which are purchased). For the taller support structures, juniper (*Juniperus* species) and false cypress (*Chamaecyparis* species) branches salvaged from material removed during winter pruning are used. To tie up shrubs and bolder perennials, the gardeners use a jute twine, but for typical perennials and annuals, they use a fine hemp string purchased at craft stores, where it is sold for stringing beads.

The secret to attractive staking is timing: you must secure the stem or stems while they are still straight, before they flop. A stem that has flopped will maintain its curved shape even when winched in and tied to a stake, and always look constricted and unhappy. Keep the stake a couple of inches lower than the growing point of the stem you are tying up, unless the plant is very fast-growing, as in the case of dahlias, in

OPPOSITE

Correct pinching and staking of asters (upper left and right) and mums (lower left and right) at the ideal times in spring and early summer encourages compact habit and a fuller blooming display, while lengthening the flowering season.

BELOW

Interwoven hoops of willow stems furnish a homegrown trellis for sweet peas to climb.

which case you draw on experience to make the stake just shorter than the ultimate height of the stems. And always secure the stem to the stake in two points at least; three is even better—a single tie creates a fulcrum point where the stem will snap.

For many-stemmed plants, the gardeners employ a variety of techniques. Peonies have metal peony rings laid over them when the shoots are just four inches tall; the rings, which come with legs attached, are raised as the stems lengthen. Plants with lots of thin stems, such as asters (*Aster* or *Symphyotrichum* species) or Culver's root (*Veronicastrum virginicum*), are simply fenced in while still young and short, using a ring of branching twigs—prunings from Japanese maples work well for this. Another way to enclose such plants is to surround them with hoops made from flexible lengths of willow or shrubby dogwood stems. Because the willows and dogwoods are grown for the winter color of their bark, their stems are harvested in spring.

For more robust, multi-stemmed plants—the hydrangea 'Annabel' in the Flower Garden, for instance—the gardeners revert to stakes and twine. They will first set six to eight bamboo stakes around the perimeter of the plant. Then they tie a length of hemp to one stake, pass the string through the stems to the opposite stake, tie it off, and pass the string back to a third stake, eventually creating a star-shaped pattern of string. Finally, they run the string in a circle around the outside of the stakes. The result is a system of support which is secure and keeps the stems from slumping together, yet is inconspicuous.

Mulching is also, for the most part, a do-it-yourself matter at Wave Hill. Instead of buying expensive, bagged products, the gardeners almost invariably make their own, chiefly from fallen autumn leaves. One- or two-year-old unchopped leaves are used to tuck in the shrubbery; this makes a durable mulch. Other leaves are chopped with a leaf shredder or lawn mower—chopped leaves from local landscapers are also accepted—and then stacked and allowed to decompose for two years, until the result is almost like peat. This serves as mulch in the Flower Garden and Herb Garden, helping to nourish the soil as the leaves finish decomposing, as well as keeping the beds weed-free, moist, and cool.

Paths are mulched with an eighth of an inch of chipped bluestone or with finely ground tree trimmings; only on the steeper paths is

OPPOSITE

A mass of tulips echo the color of flowering quince (*Chaenomeles* × *superba* 'Cameo') at the center of this view; at the arbor post to the left is a clematis with a discreet corset of recently cut, shrubby dogwood stems.

A fresh dressing of gravel makes this path a crisp divider between Japanese yew (*Taxus cuspidata*) on the right and a mixed border on the left.

ABOVE RIGHT

In the Dry Garden, gravel mulch not only serves as a unifying visual element but also enhances the growth of the plantings.

OPPOSITE

The selection of a mulch is an aesthetic, as well as practical, matter. Cinnamon-colored needles of white pine (*Pinus strobus*) provide a handsome setting for this clump of hellebores (*Helleborus atrorubens*).

store-bought shredded bark used, because it mats naturally and doesn't wash away.

A mulch of pea gravel is used in the Dry Garden and in an area of the Wild Garden where Mediterranean and arid-land plants are grown. This, spread as much as six inches deep, serves some of the same functions as an organic mulch: it insulates the soil, keeping it cooler in summertime and warmer in the fall, winter, and spring; it also helps keep the soil below moist. The gravel itself drains quickly and doesn't retain moisture, so the crowns of the plants set into it stay dry, which suits those species. A coarse sand serves a similar purpose when spread across the surface of the pots in which seeds are sown—it not only protects the seeds from disturbance when the pots are watered but also keeps the base of the emerging seedlings dry, protecting them against damping-off fungi.

Not all the decisions concerning mulches are practical. There is an aesthetic element in matching the right mulch to a plant. The Balkan hellebore *Helleborus atrorubens*, at the entrance to the Flower Garden, is mulched with the curly needles from one of the white pines on the

TOP

Crisp, neatly swept edges are the finishing touch for beds in the Flower Garden.

ABOVE

The sharp lines of a meticulously clipped hedge provide a perfect contrast for the luxuriant splendor of a Chinese wisteria (*Wisteria sinensis*) in full bloom.

OPPOSITE

As garden beds fill, mat-forming perennials are allowed to spill slightly over the line, softening the edge just a bit and giving an impression of fullness.

Smooth planes of hedges, European hornbeam (*Carpinus betulus*
'Fastigiata'), left, and western red cedar (*Thuja plicata* 'Atrovirens'), right,
echo and emphasize the ruled edge of a gravel path.

grounds, because the needles' fine texture and rust color provide such a good backdrop to the hellebore's purple-tinged flowers.

When the pressure is on to tidy the garden quickly for a party or a visit, some measures may be skimped, but not edging. A crisp, neatly swept edge is the visitor's very first impression of the garden and, as such, utterly essential. The tool used varies depending on circumstances. For edging along paths or roadsides, an experienced hand can do the job with a string trimmer held with the cutting head in a vertical position. Where stones edge a bed, sheep shears are used to clip the encroaching grass short and level. Where a bed butts right up against turf, the edge is cut with a sharp spade. Along established edges, the spade is commonly wielded freehand, but a couple of times every growing season, the edge is corrected by stretching a string between stakes and using this as a guide.

Beds and borders are edged five to six times a year, but often with a subtle change as the season progresses. The turf is always cut to a sharp edge, but as the garden beds fill up, mat-forming perennials are allowed to spill slightly over the line, softening the edge just a bit. This, explains Louis Bauer, gives "an impression of fullness."

Wave Hill Through the Seasons

PREVIOUS SPREAD

Wave Hill cycles, ever changing, through
the seasons. In early spring, glory-of-the-
snow (*Chionodoxa sardensis*) and daffodils
(*Narcissus* cultivar) create a carpet of
color around a still-dormant bald cypress
(*Taxodium distichum*) and dawn redwood
(*Metasequoia glyptostroboides*).

Gardening is often likened to painting, but really it has more in common with dance. It's true that gardeners use color, texture, and form in much the same way as do painters, and there is a similar striving to create a composition or view. But like a dance, a garden is a performance through and with time. Unlike a painting, a garden isn't static; the planting is just a beginning.

A garden interacts with time in two ways. There is the growth of the plants from day to day—and from year to year. The garden designer must envision how changes in plant sizes will affect the picture. This, while it requires some imagination, is a fairly straightforward task. Far more complex and difficult to master is the planning of the garden's relation to the cycle of the seasons. That is, the garden scene changes in its progression from winter to spring, to summer and fall, and then to winter again.

This is perhaps the greatest strength of Wave Hill. Its scenes change from day to day and week to week. The colors wax and wane, the foliage changes hue with the seasons, bursting out in spring, settling into summer, flaring in autumn, and then falling away with winter's onset to reveal the underlying sculpture of the trunks and branches. Some of the transient beauties are fortuitous, of course, but the main outlines of the seasonal displays, the transformations, are planned as carefully as a dancer works out a sequence of steps.

There is, for example, the matter of spring ephemerals, the bulbs and wildflowers that emerge to fill the Wild Garden and the Shade Border with luminous color in spring, but at that season's end go dormant, retreating back underground. This, if not planned for, could leave the gardens full of gaps. Instead, successors have been interplanted among

Glory-of-the-snow washes acres of the Wave Hill landscape in gentian-blue in season.

the ephemerals so that as these withdraw, their place is taken by later-developing plants.

In the Shade Border, the early-spring wildflowers are replaced by ferns and sedges and midspring flowers, and in turn are replaced by summer bloomers, as this pattern of succession is pursued through the rest of the growing season. Something similar happens in the Wild Garden, as the bulbs of early spring go dormant and are replaced by spring-blooming sun lovers.

Although the examples of the Shade Border and the Wild Garden are particularly dramatic as the early-spring bloomers disappear, a similar

OPPOSITE, CLOCKWISE FROM TOP LEFT

Jewels of early spring, ephemerals are welcome sights across the garden, including crocuses (*Crocus* species); wild-type tulips, such as *Tulipa kaufmanniana*; adonis (*Adonis amurensis*); species tulips and grape hyacinths (*Muscari armeniacum*).

ABOVE

Hybrid tulips and Siberian bugloss (*Brunnera macrophylla*).

Prairie natives such as compass plant (*Silphium laciniatum*), front right, whorled rosinweed (*S. trifoliatum*), front center, and wholeleaf rosinweed (*S. integrifolium*), back, combine with lily 'Stargazer', behind center, to furnish midsummer color.

OPPOSITE

The magnolia bed in springtime bloom.

sort of succession takes place in all of Wave Hill's gardens. One could think of this as a series of acts, with each introducing new characters, although they are all performed on the same stages. The various acts may differ widely; the softer pastels of the spring bulbs in the Flower Garden, for instance, are replaced by warmer, more assertive colors that show up better in the stronger sunlight that comes with late spring and summer. But if each act remains true to the setting and the concept of the garden, then the whole works together as a single, coherent composition.

Different devices are used to achieve this succession of displays. In the Elliptical Garden, all of the plants are natives of North America, but this definition is interpreted broadly. In many native-plant gardens, there is an attempt to recreate a specific ecosystem, such as a Northeast woodland or a sunny northern meadow. This can limit the display to a single peak season.

Northeastern woodlands, for example, bloom principally in early spring to midspring, before the trees have leafed out to shade the forest floor and shut down growth there of all except foliage plants. Our native grasslands are more reliant on warm-season grasses and flowers, plants that make their principal growth from late spring to late summer—their peak season of bloom comes in summer.

To circumvent this limitation, the Elliptical Garden combines plants from different ecosystems, with different seasons of flowering. The spring bloomers tend to be from eastern woodlands—bluestar (*Amsonia*), for instance, which is native to open woods from Alabama to Massachusetts and Illinois, or golden Alexanders (*Zizia aptera*), which is most common in eastern woodlands and meadows. By July, however, in high summer, the bulk of the bloom is provided by prairie natives such as coneflowers (*Echinacea* cultivars), rattlesnake master

(*Eryngium yuccifolium*), and prairie ironweed (*Vernonia fasciculata*). This strategy means that the Elliptical Garden is not as ecologically homogenous as many native plants gardens, but far more sustained and exciting in its level of bloom.

Certain collections of plants make strong seasonal statements. The magnolias, which are distributed throughout the property, especially decorate early spring to midspring, though some bloom on into late spring and even summer. For almost six weeks, from late May to July, *Magnolia sieboldii*, the Oyama magnolia, bears its nodding, perfumed, four-inch cups of porcelain white with centers of scarlet stamens. *Magnolia ×wieseneri*, one of its hybrid offspring, bears similarly crimson-centered, ivory blossoms right to September.

Magnolias are just one of several seasonal collections. Viburnums are another special pleasure of the Wave Hill spring. The Burkwood viburnum (*Viburnum ×burkwoodii* 'Conoy') covers itself with flat-topped, fragrant, white flower clusters in April. And *V. lantana, V. ×rhytidophylloides*, and *V. ×carlcephalum* 'Cayuga' shine in the Shade Border in May.

Some of the collections are geographically concentrated for extra punch. The lilacs, for example, turn their location, below the Pergola on the Lower Lawn Road, into a perfumed desti-nation at the end of spring. By mixing different species and races of hybrids, the lilacs' season of bloom is extended from the usual couple of weeks to a full month.

As the lilacs pass out of bloom, the hydrangeas come into their full glory. Six different cultivars of smooth hydrangea (*Hydrangea arborescens*) flower from June to September, while a similar assortment of bracted hydrangeas (*H. involucrata*) compete for attention with their lace caps. Clematis, clambering up through neighboring shrubs, adds a second season of

OPPOSITE, CLOCKWISE FROM TOP LEFT

A tracery of star magnolia (*Magnolia stel-lata* 'Rosea') blossoms and buds against the early-spring sky; pristine flowers of Loebner magnolia (*Magnolia ×loebneri* 'Merrill'); another beauty, the saucer magnolia (*Magnolia ×soulangeana*); bigleaf magnolia (*Magnolia macrophylla*), a native of the southeastern United States, flourishes in a sheltered spot on this south-facing slope.

BELOW

Viburnums such as this Japanese snowball (*Viburnum plicatum* f. *plicatum*) are another pleasure of the Wave Hill spring.

OPPOSITE

The lilacs turn their location, situated below the
Pergola and beside the Lower Lawn, into a perfumed
destination at the end of spring.

ABOVE

By mixing different species, the lilac season is
extended to a full month. Chinese tree lilac (*Syringa
reticulata* subsp. *pekinensis*) is the last to bloom, in
early June.

Hybrid cherry *Prunus* 'Hally Jolivette' kicks off the bloom in late spring along the lilac border.

RIGHT

The lilac border in full bloom. It is designed to be viewed from atop the retaining wall to its east.

summer bloom to its hosts and contributes a delicate texture with its fuzzy, satiny, whorled seed heads that persist from summer right into winter.

Summer, early summer at least, is easy for the gardener because so many perennials bloom then. Annuals, too, come into their first flush of flowers during that season. But while reveling in summer's blossoming, Wave Hill's gardeners still have to plan ahead; late summer's intense heat will cause plants to pause in their growth and depress flowering. To cope with this, they move tropical plants from the glasshouses out into the beds and add an alternate display. This way, even when the dog days cause blooming to stall, there is still the tropicals' bold and colorful foliage to admire.

From Wave Hill's first days as a public garden, there has been deliberate planning for that often-neglected season,

autumn. Marco Polo Stufano had noted that visitorship, which lagged a bit during the hottest days of summer, shot up in the fall, and he was determined that the gardens would not disappoint this audience.

Wave Hill's magnificent trees, some over a century old, contribute a blaze of foliage colors in the fall, and they are echoed by smaller but no less vivid plants, such as the cutleaf staghorn sumac in the Wild Garden, whose leaves turn a brilliant orange in years when the autumn weather is favorable. In addition, the planting of the Flower Garden has been adjusted to ensure a full autumn blossoming. Thus, early-spring planting for spring and summertime bloom is followed by another planting in mid- to late June of dahlia tubers, gladiolus corms, and tender salvias grown as annuals, to provide late-summer and fall color. Plants are pinched back through the spring until the beginning of July, not only to encourage bushier growth but also to delay the flowering into early fall. Likewise, as noted previously, colors are included in the annual displays around the Pergola, consciously mirroring the fall foliage along the cliffs of the Palisades, and integrating that spectacular view with the garden.

Winter is a test for the gardener, but also an opportunity. It is a pitilessly honest season: when the cold weather strips away flowers and the bulk of the leaves, the garden's basic structure is revealed, for better or for worse. Architecture—and Wave Hill with its Pergola, gazebos, and arbors is rich in it—emerges from the background to make a stronger statement. Deciduous trees and shrubs are transformed as the masses of foliage fall away to expose the sinuous armature of the trunks and branches. The smooth, gray bark of a copper beech (*Fagus sylvatica* Atropurpurea Group) emphasizes the muscularity of its limbs; the dawn redwood (*Metasequoia glyptostroboides*) sheds its needles to reveal the buttressed spire of its trunk.

OPPOSITE

Tropicals such as these cannas and agapanthuses energize the gardens at midsummer when other plants flag.

BELOW

Bracted hydrangea (*Hydrangea involucrata* 'Yokudanka') provides summer-long bloom.

Autumn juxtaposes Wave Hill's brilliant autumn foliage with a view of the distant city skyline.

OPPOSITE, CLOCKWISE FROM TOP LEFT

Plantings in mid- to late June produce colors in late summer and fall, such as dahlias for the Flower Garden; Abyssinian gladiolus (*Gladiolus* 'Boone'); gladiolus; sunflowers for fall, seen here on the south slope of Glyndor House.

Evergreens, meanwhile, loom larger. Dwarf conifers punctuate the gardens with a new force, creating rhythms and patterns unique to this season. Calculated planting has set pines, spruces, and other needled giants to obscure some views—of houses just outside the boundaries of Wave Hill—and frame, enhance, and expand others. In summertime, deciduous trees block much of the vista, but leafless in winter, the trees become transparent and the landscape has a more spacious feel. The Hudson River panoramas are sweeping, dominant especially when snow erases the foreground, leaving no color except the blue of the sky and the shadows. There is a special grandeur to Wave Hill in winter.

And so the annual dance ends, only to begin again with the arrival, soon enough, of another spring. Yet every year the performance is different. Because Louis Bauer encourages initiative and creativity among the staff, plants are always being added and subtracted or rearranged,

Winter strips the leaves and reveals the fruits of *Idesia polycarpa*; of this, the renowned English garden designer and writer Rosemary Verey wrote that the "bunches of berries were spectacular against a clear-blue winter sky."

RIGHT

The smooth, gray bark of a venerable copper beech (*Fagus sylvatica* Atropurpurea Group) introduces a tactile note.

Wave Hill Through the Seasons

By offering touches of similar colors in the garden landscape, the Pergola area echoes the scenery of the autumnal Palisades.

experiments in design are continually being conducted. The views across the Hudson River are timeless, but the gardens change.

In many respects, the changes at Wave Hill reflect changes in the world around it. As the climate shifts, for example, the bloom of familiar plants may come earlier in the spring and persist later in the fall. Summers become more intense; winters less predictable. A more violent storm or an imported pest takes down a venerable shrub or tree. New plantings, different plantings, must arise in their place.

Rare deciduous conifers, bald cypresses turn salmon-colored before dropping their needles in late fall.

ABOVE LEFT

Fall foliage colors the gardens in fall.

This process of cause and effect reflects a basic truth of gardening: that this craft is above all a means of relating to nature. Every gardener at whatever stage of experience needs to learn and respect this, which is another lesson that Wave Hill has to teach. For if we do not learn to treat nature with more respect and intelligence, not only will we be unsuccessful as gardeners, our very future is questionable. Indeed, it is no coincidence that one of Wave Hill's major institutional missions is environmental education, especially with respect to reaching out to young people.

Magnificent trees, like this centuries-old elm (seen here in summer, fall, and winter), punctuate and define the Wave Hill landscape.

Wave Hill is a masterpiece, then, but also a perpetual work in progress. Over the last 50 years, this living landscape transformed American gardening. It continues to do so today. Former home to the wealthy and famous, to artists, ambassadors, and financiers, Wave Hill has an illustrious past as a private estate. It is as a public institution, though, a place for everyone, a place to be refreshed and uplifted and to learn, that is its present and its future. A present and a future even brighter than its past.

OPPOSITE

A perpetual work in progress, Wave Hill is now a place open to all, a place to feel refreshed and uplifted.

BELOW

Snow erases all color, except the sky-blues and shadows.

NEXT SPREAD

Winter renders the deciduous trees and shrubs transparent, enhancing the role of the evergreens.

Further Reading

Ballard, Ernesta Drinker. 1974. *Growing Plants Indoors: A Garden in Your House*. New York: Barnes and Noble Books.

Brickell, Christopher. 2012. *Encyclopedia of Gardening*. New York: DK Publishing.

Brickell, Christopher and Dr. H. Marc Cathey, eds. 2004. *American Horticultural Society A–Z Encyclopedia of Garden Plants*. New York: DK Publishing.

Čapek, Karel. 2002. *The Gardener's Year*. New York: Modern Library/ Random House.

Charlesworth, Geoffrey. 1988. *The Opinionated Gardener: Random Offshoots from an Alpine Garden*. Boston: David R. Godine.

Chips, Lori. 2018. *Hypertufa Containers: Creating and Planting an Alpine Trough Garden*. Portland, Oregon: Timber Press.

Dirr, Michael. 2009. *Manual of Woody Landscape Plants: Their Identification, Ornamental Characteristics, Culture, Propagation and Uses*. Champaign, Illinois: Stipes Publishing.

Druse, Ken. 2015. *The New Shade Garden: Creating a Lush Oasis in the Age of Climate Change*. New York: Abrams Books.

Hightshoe, Gary L. 1988. *Native Trees Shrubs, and Vines for Urban and Rural America: A Planting Design Manual for Environmental Designers*. Hoboken, New Jersey: John Wiley and Sons.

Johnson, Hugh. 1979. *The Principles of Gardening: The Classic Guide to the Gardener's Art*. New York: Simon and Schuster.

Lloyd, Christopher. 1983. *The Adventurous Gardener*. New York: Random House.

Page, Russell. 2007. *The Education of a Gardener*. New York: New York Review Books Classics.

Perényi, Eleanor. 2002. *Green Thoughts: A Writer in the Garden*. New York: Vintage Books/Random House.

Sternberg, Guy. 2004. *Native Trees for North American Landscapes*. Portland, Oregon: Timber Press.

Wyman, Donald. 1987. *Wyman's Gardening Encyclopedia*. New York: Scribner.

Acknowledgments

As an author, I know that almost every book represents a collaboration between the writer and all the other people involved in bringing the text to life. This present work is, perhaps, more a collaboration than most.

First, I would like to thank Karen Meyerhoff, president and executive director of Wave Hill, whose enthusiasm and steadfast support have fueled this project from the start. Every writer should have such a patron.

I also owe an enormous debt to Louis Bauer, Wave Hill's senior director of horticulture. He proved not only endlessly patient in answering questions about his charge, but also wonderfully articulate and quotable. His philosophy of gardening fills every page of this book.

Nor could this book have been written without the shared experiences and insights of Wave Hill's gardeners: Albert Cabrera, Jennifer Cimino, Shane Pritchett, Gelene Scarborough, Harnek Singh, Susannah Strazzera, and Assistant Director of Horticulture Matthew Turnbull. They, too, always found time to answer yet another question, and were always generous with their knowledge. Their collective expertise is what makes Wave Hill the wonder it is, and we are all fortunate that they are willing to share so selflessly the knowledge that they have acquired through decades of hard work.

Charles Day, Wave Hill's Ruth Rea Howell Senior Horticultural Interpreter, seemed unstumpable as well as tireless when it came to identifying plants, and Marilyn Young, horticulture assistant, proved superb at sorting out problems and providing backup. Thanks, too, to Martha Gellens, who swept through the manuscript with a keen editorial eye, and to Rachel Morris, who wrangled the thousands of new photographs with precise organization.

I have come to understand these gardens in a new way thanks to photographer Ngoc Minh Ngo. To see Wave Hill through her eyes has been a revelation. Her work will add immeasurably to the pleasure and enlightenment readers will find in this book.

Wave Hill owes its existence to the vision and dedication of Marco Polo Stufano, its founding director of horticulture, who saw the potential of a neglected private estate and, over a period of 34 years, turned it into the most dynamic public garden in the United States. He, too, was most patient in providing information and answering questions, and remarkably tactful in redirecting my footsteps when I strayed off the path.

Again, my sincere thanks to all.

Photography Credits

All photographs are by Ngoc Minh Ngo, except the following:

pages 10, 13 top and bottom, 14 top and center, 168, 169: Wave Hill Public Garden and Cultural Center archives

page 14, bottom: Maggy Geiger

pages 21 top and bottom, 33: Marco Polo Stufano

Index

"$16.30 Garden", 32, 35

Abutilon 'Clementine', 229
Abyssinian gladiolus, 128, 272
Acacia baileyana, 220
Acacia baileyana var. purpurea, 218
acclimating plants, 82
Acer species, 101
Achillea filipendulina
        'Schwellenburg', 180
acid-loving plants, 110
Acorus calamus 'Variegatus', 83, 86
Actaea pachypoda, 108
Actinidia arguta, 200
ADA accessibility, 26
Adiantum peruvianum, 231
Adiantum venustum, 112
adonis, 261
Aeonium arboreum var.
        atropurpureum, 233
Aeonium lindleyi var. viscatum, 233
Aeonium 'Tricolor', 233
Aesculus parviflora, 26, 101
African lily, 42
Agapanthus africanus, 42
Agastache scrophulariifolia, 206
agaves, 52, 223
Alcantarea 'Malbec', 79
Alcea rosea, 45, 132
allium / Allium species, 17, 58, 66, 126
        'Early Emperor', 63, 64
Allium nigrum, 193
Allium tanguticum, 128
Allium tuberosum, 145
almond trees, 29
Alocasia macrorrhiza
        'Lutea', 78
        Portodora', 78
alocasias, 78
Alocasia wentii, 78
Alpine House
        crevices as growing spots, 148
        cultivating alpines, 151–152
        expanded definition of alpines,
                152–153
        hypertufa troughs, 148, 153–154,
                157–160, 163
        miniatures, 148, 154, 157, 160,
                163, 164
amaranth, 188
Amaranthus caudatus 'Green
        Cascade', 188

Amaranthus cruentus 'Golden
        Giant', 188
Amelanchier canadensis, 108
American elm, 26
American holly, 208
American lotus, 83
American wisteria, 211
Ammi majus, 51
Ammi visnaga, 51
Amsonia, 262
        'Blue Ice', 108
Andean silver-leaf sage, 69
Andropogon gerardii, 78
Anemone × lipsiensis, 141
annual plantings
        advantage of impermanence, 191
        bed preparation, 243
        in containers, 196–197
        expanded definition of annuals,
                188, 190
        perennials grown as, 188, 190
        self-seeding, 35, 128, 132, 179
        themed displays, 200–201
        tropical plants in annual beds,
                193, 194, 196
        vegetables, 191, 193
        winter annuals, 97
        See also Kate French Terrace;
                Paisley Bed
aphids, 231
Aquatic Garden
        caring for aquatics, 87
        containers / pots, 85–88
        overwintering, 87, 88
        pool, 72, 81, 83, 85, 87, 89
Aquilegia canadensis, 122
Aquilegia species, 21, 154
arbor, 115
arborvitaes, 61, 62, 70, 73, 75, 77, 113
architectural elements
        framing, 62, 88
        in garden design, 15, 58, 61–62,
                240
        settings, 194, 200
        structures, 39, 44, 271
architectural plants, 39, 44, 154, 220,
                223, 231
architecture vs. form, 62
Argemone mexicana, 179
arisaema / Arisaema species, 106, 108
Arisaema ringens, 103
Arisaema triphyllum, 103

Aristolochia macrophylla, 88
Asarum canadense, 101, 103
aster / Aster species, 29, 145, 244,
                247, 249
        "Chicago Bus Stop", 19
astilbe / Astilbe species, 244
Athyrium nipponicum var. pictum, 101
auricula primrose, 151
Aurinia saxatilis, 143
autumn
        deliberate planning for, 26, 268,
                271
        hues, 197, 199, 202
        vistas, 54, 69, 110, 112, 272

bald cypresses, 258, 277
bamboo stakes, 247, 249
banana, 75
        'Truly Tiny', 227
baneberry, 108
Baptisia species, 247
barrel cactus, 223
basket grass, 78
basket-of-gold, 143
Bauer, Louis
        education and background, 15, 25
        gardening philosophy, 15, 19, 52,
                54, 62, 170, 171, 185
        management style, 25, 276
        role in design, 25, 26, 92, 191, 193
bay laurel, 172
bed edges, 252, 255
bed preparation, 243–244
beeches, 98
begonia 'Starry Nights', 200
Bellis perennis, 199
Berberis thunbergii, 62
        'Aurea', 62
berries, 108
biennials, 36, 47, 54, 128, 132
big bluestem, 78
bindweed, 122
bishop's hat, 101
bishop's weed, 51
blackberry lily, 75
black cherry, 12
bleeding heart, 103, 105
bloodleaf, 199
bloom, succession of, 25–26, 52, 179,
                258–259, 262, 265, 271, 272
bloom season, extending, 103, 244,
                247, 262, 265, 267

blue Atlas cedar, 17
blue cardinal flower, 215
blue ginger, 79
blue mistflower, 108
blue sotol, 85, 86, 88
bluestar, 262
Bolivian sage, 188
borage, 172
Borago officinalis, 172
bottlebrush buckeye, 26, 101
Bougainvillea 'Firecracker Red', 218
Bouteloua gracilis, 78
bowman's root, 206
boxwoods, 172
Bradford pear, 213
Blechnum brasiliense, 194
broadleaf arrowhead, 83
bromeliads, 79, 86, 88, 221, 227
bronze fennel, 17
brown-eyed Susan, 215
Brunnera macrophylla, 101, 261
Buddleja davidii 'Fortune', 51
bulbs, 29, 101, 193
bush clovers, 247
butterfly bush, 51
    'Pink Delight', 51
Buxus sinica var. *insularis* 'Justin
    Brouwers', 172

cabbage tree, 75
Cabrera, Albert, 63, 244
cacti, 177, 220, 223
Cactus and Succulent House,
    220–221, 223, 231, 233
Calamagrostis ×*acutiflora* 'Karl
    Foerster', 78
calamint, 66
California poppy, 52
camas, 17, 126
camassia / *Camassia*, 17, 66
Camassia leichtlinii subsp.
    suksdorfii, 126
Camellia 'Crimson Candles', 163
Camellia japonica
    'Bokuhan', 227
    'Tinsie', 227
Camellia 'Survivor', 113
Campsis radicans 'Crimson
    Trumpet', 88
Campsis radicans f. *flava*, 134
Campsis × *tagliabuana* 'Madame
    Galen', 88
candytuft, 157
canna / *Canna*, 75, 85, 86
    'Intrigue', 188
    'Le Roi Humbert', 75
    'Phasion' TROPICANNA, 42
Cape fuchsia, 45, 48
Cape leadwort, 218
cardamom, 172
cardoon, 42

Carpinus betulus 'Fastigiata', 73, 81,
    254
catalpa, 39
Catalpa bignonioides 'Aurea', 48
cedars, 17
Cedrus atlantica 'Glauca Pendula',
    17, 128
Cedrus brevifolia 'Treveron', 148
Ceratostigma plumbaginoides, 108
Chaenomeles × *superba* 'Cameo, 249
Chamaecrista fasciculata, 215
Chamaecyparis pisifera 'Filifera
    Aurea', 61
Chamaecyparis species, 247
checkered lily, 141
cherry, 29, 268
Chilean iris, 78
Chinese indigo, 171
Chinese tree lilac, 267
Chinese wild gingers, 106
Chinese wisteria, 211, 252
Chionodoxa sardensis, 258
chir pine, 148
chrysanthemum / *Chrysanthemum*
    species and hybrids, 66, 244
Chrysopogon zizanioides, 172
Cimino, Jen, 76, 78, 81–82, 85–86,
    197, 201
clary sage, 172
clasping heliotrope, 69
clematises, 36, 39, 137, 249, 265, 268
Clematis integrifolia, 36
Clematis montana var. *rubens*, 137
Clematis tibetana, 52
Clematis × *triternata*
    'Rubromarginata', 36
clerodendrum, 229
Clerodendrum incisum, 229
climate, 11, 13, 19, 21, 26, 276–277
Clivia miniata, 227
Cobaea scandens, 172, 175
cobra lilies, 108
Cocos nucifera, 75
Coelogyne orchid, 225
coleus, 199, 223, 244
Colocasia esculenta 'Red Rhubarb', 79
Colocasia species, 85
color
    autumn hues, 197, 199, 202
    complementary contrasts, 63,
        66, 191
    form vs., 15
    from fruits, 108, 109
    monochromatic palettes, 58–59,
        61, 69
    plant / scenery integration,
        199–200, 276
    themed displays, 36
    unconventional, 44–45
Colour in My Garden (Wilder), 59

columbines, 122, 154, 159
compass plant, 262
compost, 110, 169, 177, 196, 243
coneflowers, 42, 215, 244, 262
conifers, 26, 61, 272, 277
Conoclinium coelestinum, 108
Conservatory
    as backdrop, 35
    Cactus and Succulent House,
        220–221, 223, 231, 233
    Palm House, 218, 225, 227, 231, 233
    Propagation House, 223, 233, 234
    scale, 234, 237
    Tropical House, 79, 81, 221, 223,
        227, 233
    winter use, 23, 218, 220
    See also glasshouses
Consolida ajacis, 41
containers / pots
    aquatic plants, 85–87, 85–88
    clay, 227, 233, 240, 241
    clustered, 196–197, 218
    as focal points, 196
    as garden statuary, 81
    hanging, 199
    hypertufa troughs, 148, 153–154,
        157–160, 163
    "Long Toms", 151
    overwintering, 87, 88
    potting mix, 196, 228
    potting of plants, 240–241
    for starting seeds, 242
    themed, 175
Convolvulus arvensis, 122
copper beech, 271, 274
coral bells, 206, 244
Cordyline australis, 75
coreopsis / *Coreopsis*, 66, 128
    'Polaris', 66
    'Snowberry', 66
Coreopsis verticillata, 128
Cornus controversa 'Variegata', 26
Cornus sanguinea 'Midwinter Fire', 29
Cornus species, 249
Cosmos sulphureus 'Tango', 177
Costus malortieanus, 75
Cotinus coggygria 'Royal Purple', 40
cotoneaster, 109
Cotoneaster salicifolius var. *rugosus*,
    109
Cottage Residences (Downing), 190
cotton, 171
creeping broom, 154
creeping evergreen euonymus, 62
crevices as growing spots, 148, 153, 159
Crocosmia
    'Emberglow', 79
    'Lucifer', 79
crocus / *Crocus* species, 66, 101, 261
Culver's root, 249
cup and saucer vine, 172, 175

Curcuma longa, 174
cutleaf staghorn sumac, 120, 121, 145, 271
Cynara cardunculus, 42
Cyperus alternifolius 'Variegatus', 85
Cyperus papyrus, 87
Cyperus species, 85
cypress vine, 86
Cyprus cedar, 148

daffodils, 258
dahlia / *Dahlia*
    'Bednall Beauty', 40
    'Classic Elise', 42
    'Daydreamer', 49
    'Japanese Bishop', 51
    'Robin Hood', 42
    staking, 247, 249
    tubers, 47, 271, 272
Daphne genkwa, 61
Darmera peltata, 98
Dasylirion berlandieri, 85, 86
Daucus carota 'Dara', 51
dawn redwood, 258, 271
daylilies, 61, 66, 75, 244
deadheading, 245, 247
Delany, Mary, 83, 85
Delosperma cooperi, 175
Delosperma sutherlandii, 180
delphinium / *Delphinium* species, 244
Deno, Norman C., 209
desertbells, 220
dianthus, 154, 159
Dianthus barbatus 'Heart Attack', 44
Dianthus simulans, 154
Dichorisandra thyrsiflora, 79
Digitalis grandiflora, 132
Digitalis purpurea, 132, 171
Digitalis species, 21, 47, 244
Digitalis trojana
Dipsacus fullonum, 174
Disporum flavens, 105
dogwood, 29, 139, 249
Downing, Andrew Jackson, 190
Dracaena reflexa, 78
drainage
    amending soil, 125, 151, 177, 243–244
    overwintering and, 185
    site-enhanced, 160, 168, 185
    troughs, 157, 159
Dry Garden
    containers / pots, 175
    development, 168–169, 171
    dryland plant irrigation, 174–175, 177, 179
    foliage, 174, 179–180, 184
    fragrances, 184–185
    microclimates, 175, 177, 185
dusty miller, 69, 188
Dutchman's pipe, 88

dwarf conifers, 26, 272
dwarf crested iris, 105
dwarf evergreens, 61, 126, 131, 153
dwarf fothergilla, 97, 103
dwarf Japanese red pine, 61
dwarf pinyon pine, 157
dwarf statice, 153
dwarf white pines, 208
dwarf willow, 157
dwarf zinnias, 179
dye plants, 171–171
dyer's broom, 171
dyer's woad, 132

eastern arborvitae, 62
    'Globosa', 61
eastern red cedars, 208
eastern white pine, 153
Echeveria pulvinata 'Frosty', 233
Echinacea cultivars, 215, 262
Echinops sphaerocephalus, 128
ecosystems, combining, 262, 265
edges, refining, 240, 252, 254, 255
education, visitor, 73, 169, 172, 281
elephant ear, 79, 85
Elettaria cardamomum, 172
Elliptical Garden, 23, 206, 208, 211–213, 215, 262, 265. *See also* native plants
elms, 26, 62, 72, 75, 77, 92
Emanuel, John, 23
Enkianthus campanulatus 'Red Bells', 19
enkianthus / *Enkianthus* species, 103
Ensete ventricosum 'Maurelii', 79
Epimedium grandiflorum, 101
epiphytic plants, 223, 227, 229
eremurus, 66
Erigeron species, 154
Eryngium planum, 41, 128
Eryngium yuccifolium, 262
Erysimum 'Apricot Sunset', 52
Erythronium americanum, 103
Eschscholzia californica 'Copper Pot', 52
espalier, 211, 212
Eucalyptus cinerea, 218
Eucomis comosa 'Sparkling Burgundy', 19, 44
Eucomis 'Sparkling Burgundy', 44
Euonymus fortunei
    'Emerald 'n' Gold', 61, 62
    'Variegatus', 88
Euphorbia horrida 'Snowflake', 233
Euphorbia obesa, 233
euphorbias, 62, 233
European hornbeam, 81, 254
European inspiration, 15, 29, 45, 151
Eutrochium maculatum, 215
Everett, T.H., 19, 240
evergreen euonymous, 62

evergreens
    changes over time, 113, 126, 130
    design use, 272, 281
    dwarf, 61, 126, 131, 153
    root systems, 98
exotic plants, 11, 13, 97, 122, 190, 213, 218
eyelash grass, 78

Fagus sylvatica Atropurpurea Group, 271, 274
fairy bells, 105
false cypress, 247
false indigo, 247
feather reed grass, 78
fennel, 171
ferns, 101, 112, 231, 259
Ferraria crispa, 225
fertilization programs
    alpines, 152, 159, 163
    annuals, 196
    aquatics, 87
    growing lean philosophy, 231
    shade plants, 110
    succulents, 231
    tropicals, 82, 231
    troughs, 159, 163
Festuca glauca, 78
Festuca idahoensis, 78
Ficus carica, 171
figs, 171
flame azaleas, 94, 103
flame vine, 218
flax, 171
fleabane, 154
floating plants, 85
Flower Garden
    bed structure, 39, 44, 252
    color themes, 36, 39–44
    flexibility in planting, 51–52, 54
    imports, 45, 47
    rose garden conversion, 23, 32, 35–36
    succession of bloom, 52, 262, 271, 272
flowering maple, 229
flowering quince, 248
flux, state of, 125, 190–191, 276, 281
focal points, 39, 59, 171, 172, 196, 223
Foeniculum vulgare, 171
    'Purpureum', 17
foliage
    design use in monochromatic garden, 61–62, 63, 69
    fall, 19, 108–109, 199–200, 202, 272, 277
    gold, 59, 61
    shade plants, 106, 108–109
    silver, 179–180
    as star, 72, 75–76, 78–79
    textures, 174, 180, 184

forget-me-nots, 103, 159
form
    architecture vs., 62
    color vs., 15
    design use in monochromatic
        garden, 58, 61–62, 63, 66
    sculptural plants, 66, 76, 81, 223,
        237
    See also architectural elements
formality / informality tension, 89
formal plant displays, 23, 206, 208,
    211, 212
formal settings, 72, 194
Forsythia × *intermedia* hybrids, 247
forsythias, 247
Fothergilla gardenii, 97
fountain grass, 177
foxgloves, 21, 36, 47, 132, 171, 244
    Helen of Troy, 45
French marigolds, 188
Fritillaria meleagris, 141
Fritillaria pallida, 141
fruits, 19, 62, 63, 103, 108, 171, 274
fuller's teasel, 174

Galanthus species, 101
garden thyme, 171, 172
garlic, 193
gazebo, 23, 25, 118, 121, 134, 136, 144
Genista pilosa, 154
geranium / *Geranium* species, 154, 190
    'Gerwat' ROZANNE, 108
    'Tiny Monster', 108
Geranium maculatum, 105
Germination Instructions for Seeds,
    209
giant larkspur, 41
Gillenia trifoliata, 206
gladiolus corms, 47, 271, 272
gladiolus / *Gladiolus*, 19, 47, 227
    'Boone', 272
    'Carolina Primrose', 19
Gladiolus murielae, 128, 272
Gladiolus tristis var. *concolor*, 227
glasshouses
    clay pots, 227
    as focal point, 223
    renovation / repurposing, 19, 21,
        168–169, 171, 223
    role in garden functioning, 82,
        223
    temperature control, 233
globe daisy, 157
globe thistle, 128
Globularia species, 157
glory-of-the-snow, 258, 259
Glyndor House, 13
Gold border, 58–59, 61–64, 66, 69, 244
golden Alexanders, 262
golden catalpa, 39
golden hoptree, 58, 63

golden lace, 40
golden seal, 174
Gossypium herbaceum, 171
gourds, 88
grape hyacinths, 63, 162, 261
grapes
    'Concord', 88
    'Niagara', 88
grapevine tripods, 85–86
grasses, 78, 145, 177
Great Dixter, 15, 45
great white trillium, 103

habitats
    alpine, 148, 153
    cliff, 153
    diversity of, 118, 125–126, 211
    dry shade, 98
    native plants, 209
    tropical, 221
Hakonechloa macra, 245
    'All Gold', 47
Hakone grass, 245
Hall, Elizabeth, 32
Hamamelis virginiana, 109
hardiness, 174, 176
hardy kiwi, 200
Haworthia cymbiformis, 233
heath aster, 19
hedges, 73, 81, 208, 211, 252, 254
Helenium autumnale and hybrids, 244
Helen of Troy foxglove, 45
Helianthus angustifolius 'Matanzas
    Creek', 215
Helichrysum petiolare, 69
Heliopsis helianthoides 'Prairie
    Sunset', 51, 66
Heliotropium amplexicaule, 69
hellebore, 255
Helleborus atrorubens, 250
Helleborus foetidus, 5, 141
Hemerocallis species, 244
    'Autumn King', 75
    'Golden Chimes', 61
hemlock, 98
hen and chicks, 160
Hepatica acutiloba, 151
Herbert and Hyonja Abrons
    Woodland, 23, 208, 211
Herb Garden
    bed preparation, 243–244
    containers, 175
    layout, 169, 171, 172
    microclimates, 168, 169, 170–171
    self-seeding plants, 172
heuchera / *Heuchera*, 44
    'Caramel', 208
    'Mocha', 206
Hidalgo stachys, 185
Himalayan maidenhair fern, 112

history of Wave Hill, 10–11, 13–15, 19,
    21, 23
hollyhocks, 45, 132
honesty, 143
honeysuckle, 51
hoop house, 220, 233
hornbeams, 73, 81, 98, 254
hosta / *Hosta*, 101
    'Queen Josephine', 244
Hudson River and Palisades
    consideration in garden design,
        21, 23, 199–200, 202, 276
    vistas, 25, 69, 144, 160
humus, 112, 125
Hyacinthoides hispanica, 92, 105
Hydrangea arborescens, 265
Hydrangea involucrata, 265
Hydrangea paniculata, 52
Hydrangea quercifolia, 97, 108, 109
hydrangeas, 52, 97, 108, 109, 265
    'Annabel', 249
Hydrastis canadensis, 174
Hypericum tomentosum, 180
hypertufa troughs, 148, 153–154,
    157–160, 163
hyssop, 206

Iberis taurica, 157
iboza, 220
ice plant, 175, 180
Idaho fescue, 78
Idesia polycarpa, 19, 274
Ilex glabra, 208
    'Shamrock', 211
Ilex 'Rock Garden', 153
Ilex verticillata 'Winter Gold', 108, 115
India plant, 78
inkberry holly, 208, 211
invasive plants, 62, 122
in winter, 23
Ipomoea batatas, 227
Ipomoea quamoclit, 86
Iresine, 199
Iris cristata, 105
Iris domestica, 75, 78
iris / *Iris* species, 36, 52, 121, 245
    'Florentina', 121
Iris sibirica
    'Lady Vanessa', 39
    'Pansy Purple', 43
irrigation
    alpine plants, 152, 163
    clay pots, 227
    dryland plants, 174–175, 177, 179
    glasshouses, 231, 233
    in the Shade Border, 110
    tropicals, 82
Isatis tinctoria, 132

Jack-in-the-pulpit, 103
Jacobaea maritima, 188
Japanese barberry, 62
Japanese cobra lily, 103
Japanese false cypress, 61
Japanese forest grass, 47
Japanese holly, 153
Japanese maples, 249
Japanese painted fern, 101
Japanese red pine, 61, 62, 64, 69
Japanese spicebush, 94
Japanese wisteria, 211
Japanese yew, 250
jasmine, 180
Jasminum officinale, 180
Jerusalem sage, 69
Joe Pye weed, 215
jonquils, 162
junipers, 179, 180, 247
Juniperus chinensis 'Shimpaku', 157
Juniperus species, 180, 247
Juniperus virginiana, 208

Kate French Terrace, 193–194,
    196–197, 201, 243
Kentucky wisteria 'Blue Moon', 212,
    213
Kirengeshoma palmata, 103, 106
kiwi, 200
Knautia macedonica, 128
kniphofia / *Kniphofia* species, 62, 179
Kniphofia uvaria 'Echo Yellow', 58
kohleria / *Kohleria* species, 229
    'Rebecka', 229
Korean fir, 148

Lady Banks rose, 218
Lamprocapnos spectabilis 'Alba',
    103, 105
laurustinus, 227
lavandin, 180
Lavandula ×intermedia 'Grosso', 180
lavenders, 170, 171, 179, 180, 185, 243
layering, 75, 134, 137–139
Layia gaillardioides, 194
lemon grass, 174
Lespedeza species, 247
lettuces, 177, 193, 196
    'Really Red Deer Tongue', 194
Libertia ixioides 'Goldfinger', 78
licorice plant, 69
licorice weed, 197
lilac daphne, 61
lilacs, 265, 267, 268
Lilium henryi var. *citrinum*, 79
Lilium longiflorum, 79
Lilium martagon, 79
lily 'Stargazer', 262
limber pine, 131
Lindera benzoin, 108
Lindera obtusiloba, 94

Linum usitatissimum, 171
Liquidambar styraciflua, 12, 108
    'Gum Ball', 109
Lobelia siphilitica, 215
Lonicera periclymenum 'Graham
    Thomas', 51
lotus, 73, 83, 85, 86, 87
love-in-a-mist, 21
Ludwigia sedioides, 83
Lunaria Annua, 143

magnolia / *Magnolia* species, 101,
    262, 265
    Oyama, 265
Magnolia sieboldii, 265
magnolia vine, 88
Magnolia × wieseneri, 265
maples, 98, 101
Marco Polo Stufano Conservatory.
    See Conservatory
marsh mallow, 172
martagon lily, 48
masterwort, 51
mayapples, 106
medicinal plants, 171
Mediterranean and arid-land plants,
    250
Mediterranean-type microclimates,
    168, 169, 175, 177
Mediterranean upland effect, 138, 143
Mertensia virginica, 103, 143
Metasequoia glyptostroboides, 258, 271
Mexican feather grasses, 180
Mexican mint, 174
Mexican prickly poppies, 179
Mexican speckled wandering Jew, 75
microclimates
    maximizing, 170–171, 185
    Mediterranean type, 168, 169,
        175, 177
milk thistle, 172
Millard, Albert, 10, 118
miniatures, 148, 154, 157, 160, 163, 164
mock oranges, 247
mondo grass, 79
Monocot Garden, 72–73, 75–79, 81
monocots, defined, 73
Monolena primuliflora, 229
Monstera deliciosa, 75
moon carrot, 180
mosaic plant, 83
moss phlox, 208, 211
Muhlenbergia capillaris, 179
muhlygrass, 179, 180
mulch and mulching
    aesthetic aspects, 250, 255
    gravel, 179, 250
    leaves, 98, 101, 112, 115, 249
    paths, 249–250
    pea gravel, 250
mullein, 132

mums, 247
Musa
    'Siam Beauty', 75
    'Truly Tiny', 75
    Musa basjoo, 79
Muscari armeniacum, 261
Muscari latifolia, 63
Muscari neglectum, 162
mustard 'Golden Streaks', 194
Myosotis scorpioides, 103
Myriophyllum species, 85

Nally, John
    "Chicago Bus Stop" aster, 19
    education and background, 15
    European travel, 14, 15, 45
    role in design, 15, 21, 23, 32,
        35–36, 73, 89, 121
    straight species planting, 125
Narcissus cultivars, 143, 258
Narcissus jonquilla, 162
Narcissus poeticus, 63
narrowleaf cattail, 83
Nassella tenuissima, 180
nasturtiums, 52, 172
natal lily, 227
native plants
    Asian ancestry, 101, 103, 106, 174
    bloom level, 262, 265
    formal displays, 23, 206, 208,
        211, 212
    in home gardens, 206, 208, 209
    insects and, 211, 213
    Old World / New World, 101, 220,
        221, 223, 231
    prairie natives, 215, 262
    starting from seed, 209, 242
    trees, 97, 213
neillia / *Neillia* species, 247
Nelumbo 'Green Maiden', 86
Nelumbo lutea, 83
Nelumbo nucifera, 73, 83, 87
Nepeta calamintha 'Blue Cloud', 66
Neptunia aquatica, 85
New York Botanical Garden, 19, 148,
    151, 206, 240
New York ironweed, 215
New Zealand flax, 52, 78
Nigella damascena, 21
North American Rock Garden
    Society, 209
North American trilliums, 106
Nymphaea cultivars, 83
    'Foxfire', 83
Nymphoides peltata, 83

oakleaf hydrangeas, 97, 108, 109
oaks, 97, 98, 213
Ocimum basilicum, 174
Olea europaea, 172
olive trees, 172

Olmsted Brothers, 122
Ophiopogon planiscapus 'Ebony
   Knight', 79
Oplismenus hirtellus 'Variegatus', 78
Opuntia humifusa, 177
ornamental onions, 17, 128
ornamental peppers, 172
ornamental sages, 54
ornamental sweet potatoes, 227
Oryza sativa 'Red Dragon', 86
Oudolf, Piet, 63, 65
overcup oak, 97
Oxalis obtusa 'Tangerine', 162, 163
ox-eye sunflower, 51, 60, 66, 69

Paisley Bed, 188, 190–191, 193, 196,
   200, 243
Palisades cliffs. *See* Hudson River
   and Palisades
Palm House, 218, 225, 227, 231, 233
panicle hydrangea, 52
Papaver somniferum, 21
Papaver species, 172
"paper mosaics", 83, 85
papyrus, 83, 87
parrot feather, 85, 88
Parrotia persica, 245
parrotia trees, 23, 25
parsley, 174, 177
partridge pea, 215
passionflower, 229
Patrinia scabiosifolia 'Nagoya', 40
pea family, 247
Pelargonium × *hortorum*, 188
Pennisetum setaceum 'Rubrum', 177
peonies, 36, 249
Pergola, 188, 197, 199, 200–202, 267,
   271, 276
pergolas, 72, 88, 171
Perkins, George W., 10
Perkins family, 13–14
Persian ironwood tree, 245
Persicaria amplexicaulis 'Summer
   Dance', 144
Persicaria tinctoria, 171
Peruvian maidenhair fern, 231
Petroselinum crispum, 174, 177
Peucedanum ostruthium 'Daphnis',
   51
Phacelia campanularia, 220
pheasant-eye narcissus, 63
Phemeranthus calycinus, 179
Philadelphus species, 247
Phlomis fruticosa, 69
phlox, 105, 208, 211, 244
Phlox divaricata, 105, 211
Phlox kelseyi, 153
Phlox paniculata, 244
Phlox subulata, 157, 208
   'Emerald Cushion Blue', 211

Phormium tenax
   'Jester', 52
   'Radiance', 78
Phygelius, 45
Phygelius capensis, 48
pickerel weed, 83, 87
pinching, 244–245, 271
pincushion flower, 148
pineapple lily, 19
Pinus densiflora 'Umbraculifera',
   61, 64
Pinus edulis 'Farmy', 157
Pinus flexilis 'Glauca Prostrata', 131
Pinus strobus 'Nana', 208
   Pinus strobus 'Horsford', 153
pinyon pine, 157
Pistia stratiotes, 85
pitcher plants, 85, 86
"plants first" philosophy, 15
Plectranthus amboinicus, 174
Plectranthus scutellarioides, 223, 244
Plectranthus species, 223
   'Kiwi Fern', 199
plumbago, 108
Plumbago auriculata, 218
Podophyllum hexandrum, 106
Podophyllum peltatum, 106
Podophyllum pleianthum, 106
polygonum, 145
pomegranate, 171
Pontederia cordata, 83, 87
poor man's orchid, 194
poppies, 21, 51, 66, 172
Porteranthus trifoliatus, 206
prairie ironweed, 262
primrose, 151
Primula auricula 'Blue Velvet', 151
Primula bulleyana, 98
Pritchett, Shane, 193, 201
propagation
   cuttings, 15, 19
   dividing, 87
   starting seeds, 14, 32, 209, 234, 242
   See also self-seeding plants
Propagation House, 233, 234
Prunus cerasifera 'Atropurpurea',
   40–41
Prunus 'Hally Jolivette', 268
Prunus serotina, 12
Ptelea trifoliata 'Aurea', 58, 63
Pulmonaria 'Diana Clare', 63
Punica granatum, 171
purple bell vine, 227
purple-flowering raspberry, 206
Pyrostegia venusta, 218
Pyrus calleryana 'Bradford', 213

Queen Anne's lace, 51
Quercus alba, 213
Quercus lyrata, 97

rattlesnake master, 262
red banana, 79, 82
redvein enkianthus, 19
Rhodochiton atrosanguineus, 227
Rhododendron calendulaceum, 94,
   103, 105
Rhododendron 'Colin Kendrick', 143
rhododendron / *Rhododendron*
   species, 101
Rhus typhina 'Laciniata', 120, 121
rhythms, visual, 44, 62, 79, 196, 272
Robinson, William, 122
rock pink, 179
rondel, 52
Rosa banksiae 'Alba-Plena', 218
rose garden conversion, 23, 32, 35–36
rosemary, 175
'Rose Queen' bishop's hat, 101
roses
   'Alchymist', 39
   climbing, 39, 45
   'Mary Wallace', 39
   'Silver Moon', 36
   'Veilchenblau', 39, 41
rosinweed, 262
Rosmarinus officinalis, 175
Rossbach Monocot Garden, 72–73,
   75–79, 81
Royal Botanic Gardens, 14, 125, 151,
   240
Rubus odoratus, 207
Rudbeckia maxima, 42
Rudbeckia species, 244
Rudbeckia triloba, 215

Saccharum officinarum 'Pele's
   Smoke', 79
Sackville-West, Vita, 58
sacred lotus, 83, 85, 87
sages, 179
Sagittaria latifolia, 83
Salix repens 'Boyd's Pendula', 157
Salvia discolor, 69
Salvia greggii, 175
Salvia guaranitica 'Amistad', 51
Salvia oxyphora, 188
salvia / *Salvia*, 47, 179, 271
   'Royal Bumble', 40
   'Waverly', 54
Salvia sclarea, 172
sand, 151, 164, 250
Sanguisorba officinalis, 40
Sarracenia flava 'Cut Throat', 86
Sarracenia flava var. *flava*, 85
Sarracenia flava var. *ornata* 'LW5', 85
Sarracenia flava var. *rugelii*, 85
Saruma henryi, 106
Sauromatum venosum, 106
Scabiosa japonica var. *alpina* 'Ritz
   Blue', 148
Scarborough, Gelene, 122, 125, 172, 177

Schisandra glaucescens, 88
Schizanthus pinnatus, 194
Scoparia dulcis 'Illumina Lemon Mist', 197
skullcap, 206
Scutellaria galericulata, 206
sea holly, 41, 128
seasons
    changing views, 26, 278
    incorporating in design, 134, 137, 258
    seasonal collections, 265, 267–268
    spring vistas, 143, 191, 258, 262, 267, 268
    summer vistas, 26, 72, 81, 237
    winter vistas, 26, 113, 218, 271–272, 274, 281
    See also autumn
sedges, 259
Seed Germination Theory and Practice (Deno), 209
seeds, distribution programs, 125
seeds, starting, 14, 32, 209, 234, 242
self-seeding plants
    aggressive spreaders, 113, 172
    annuals, 35, 128, 132, 179
    appearance, 128, 132
    editing, 19, 112–113, 128, 132, 134
    herbs, 172
    institutional memory, 25
    role in design, 19, 21, 35, 128
Sempervivum arachnoideum, 160
Senecio viravira, 69
sensitive plant, 85
shadbush, 108
Shade Border
    changing character, 113
    color, 108–109
    degrees of light, 92, 94, 97
    development and layout, 92
    dry and moist shade, 98, 101
    foliage, 106, 108, 245
    planting and care, 110, 112–113
    spring bloomers as mainstay, 101, 103, 105–106
    succession of bloom, 258–259
    weeding and editing, 112–113
shakkei, 199
sharp-lobed hepatica, 151
shooting star, 141
Siberian bugloss, 101, 113, 261
Siberian iris, 43
Silene armeria, 179
Silphium integrifolium, 262
Silphium laciniatum, 262
Silphium trifoliatum, 262
silver dollar tree, 218
Singh, Harnek, 36, 47, 51, 52
site of Wave Hill, 10–11, 13–14, 118
smokebush, 40
sneezeweed, 244

snowdrops, 101
soil
    alpine mix, 151–152
    amending for drainage, 125, 151, 177, 243–244
    annuals, 196
    bed preparation, 243–244
    nutrient-poor, 169, 177
    pasteurization, 177
    pH, 110
    potting mix, 196, 228
    seed-starting mix, 242
    shady conditions, 98, 110
South African sand lily, 227
Spanish bluebells, 92, 105
Spanish moss, 89
spicebush, 108
spider iris, 225
Spigelia marilandica, 108
spiraea / *Spiraea* species, 247
spruce, 98
spurflowers, 223
staff, horticultural
    argumentative process, 23, 25
    institutional craft, 240–241, 243
    institutional memory, 25
    specialization, 25
    See also individual names
staking, 244, 247, 249
statice, 153
stepladder ginger, 75
stinking hellebore, 5
St. John's wort, 180
straight species planting, 125
Strazzera, Susannah, 98, 110, 157
Stufano, Marco Polo
    education and background, 15, 32, 148, 190, 206, 208
    European travel, 14–15, 45, 151
    gardening philosophy, 15, 19, 44–45, 54, 61–62, 151, 234
    glasshouses project, 19, 21, 168
    role in design, 23, 25, 32, 35–36, 73–74, 168–169, 191, 208
    straight species planting, 125
succulents
    drought and growth pattern, 220–221
    New World / Old World, 220, 221, 223, 231
    sculptural forms, 81, 223
sugar cane, 79
sugar maple, 26, 62
sulfur cosmos, 177
summer phlox, 244
sunflowers, 51, 66, 69, 215, 272
sunlight
    degrees of, 92, 94, 97
    exposure and site selection, 170
    shifting patterns of, 126, 130
swamp sunflower, 215

sweet basil, 174
sweet flag, 86
sweet gum trees, 12, 108, 109
sweet peas, 247
sweet William, 44
sweet William silene, 179
Swiss cheese plant, 75
Symphyotrichum ericoides, 19
Symphyotrichum species, 144, 244, 249
Syringa reticulata subsp. *pekinensis*, 267

Tagetes patula, 188
Tallamy, Douglas W., 213
Taxodium distichum, 258
Taxus cuspidata, 250
tea viburnum, 63
Tetradenia riparia, 220
T.H. Everett Alpine House. *See* Alpine House
The Wild Garden (Robinson), 122
threadleaf coreopsis, 128
Thuja occidentalis, 113
Thuja plicata 'Atrovirens', 254
Thymus vulgaris, 171, 172
tickseed, 66
Tillandsia usneoides, 89
Tinantia pringlei, 75
torch lilies, 58, 179
A Treatise on the Theory and Practice of Landscape Gardening (Downing), 190
trees
    changes over time, 113
    deciduous, 94, 97, 101, 271, 272, 277, 281
    design use, 75, 278
    exotic species, 97
    native, 97, 213
    roots and soil conditions, 98, 110
    in winter, 271–272, 274, 281
trellises, 45, 85–86
Trillium cuneatum, 108
Trillium erectum, 103, 108
Trillium grandiflorum, 103, 108
Trillium sessile, 103, 108
trillium / *Trillium* species, 101, 103, 106, 108
Tropical House, 79, 81, 221, 223, 227, 229, 233
tropical plants
    caring for, 82, 228, 231, 233
    summer displays, 21, 23, 79, 81, 268, 271
    use in annual beds, 193, 194, 196
troughs, 148, 153–154, 157–160, 163
trout lilies, 103
trumpet vines, 88, 134
Tulipa batalinii 'Bright Gem', 52
Tulipa kaufmanniana, 261
Tulipa sylvestris, 141

tulips, 141, 142, 194, 248
    'Juan', 193
    species tulips, 138, 143, 179, 261
turmeric, 174
tuteurs, 39, 41, 44, 45
Twain, Mark, on Wave Hill, 11
Typha angustifolia, 83

Ulmus americana, 26, 92
umbels, 51
umbrella Japanese red pine, 69
umbrella plant, 85, 98
understory planting, 92, 97
upright wild ginger, 2, 106

variegated corn, 75, 231
variegated euonymus, 47, 61
variegated giant dogwood, 26
variegated Japanese butterbur, 98
variegated masterwort, 47
variegated sweet flag, 83
variegated umbrella plant, 85
vegetables, 191, 193
Veltheimia capensis var. *rosea*, 227
Veratrum nigrum, 78
Verbascum species, 132
Verbena bonariensis, 45
verbenas, 190
Vernonia fasciculata, 262
Vernonia noveboracensis, 215
Veronicastrum virginicum, 249
verticality, 45
vetiver, 172
Viburnum × *burkwoodii* 'Conoy', 265
Viburnum × *carlcephalum* 'Cayuga', 265
Viburnum dilatatum, 108
Viburnum lantana, 108, 265
Viburnum × *rhytidophylloides*, 108
Viburnum setigerum, 63
Viburnum tinus, 227
viburnum / *Viburnum* species, 63, 66, 101, 108, 265
    Burkwood, 265
    'Cayuga', 108
views
    framing and integrating, 197, 199–200, 202
    manipulating, 23, 118, 132, 134, 139, 144
    obscuring and enhancing, 272
violas, 194
    'Sorbet Orchid Rose Beacon', 194
Virginia bluebells, 103, 138, 143
visitor education, 73, 169, 172, 281
voodoo lily, 106, 108

wallflowers, 52
watering. *See* irrigation
water lettuce, 85, 88
water lilies, 83, 85, 87

Wave Hill House, 13
Went's hardy elephant ear, 78
western red cedar, 254
white oak, 213
white pine, 208, 250
wholeleaf rosinweed, 262
whorled rosinweed, 262
wild carrot, 51
Wilder, Louise Beebe, 58
wildflowers, 101, 258, 259
Wild Garden
    changeability, 125–126, 128, 144
    development, 118, 121–122, 125
    editing, 128, 132, 134
    gazebo, 23, 25, 118, 121, 134, 136, 144
    maintenance, 144
    manipulation of views, 23, 25, 118, 132, 134
    role of self-seeding plants, 19, 128
    soil, 243
wild ginger, 101, 103
Wild Ones, 209
willows, 29, 157, 247, 249
windflower, 141
winds, 11, 13
winterberry, 108, 115
wintercreeper, 88
Wisteria floribunda, 211
Wisteria macrostachya 'Blue Moon', 211
Wisteria sinensis, 211, 252
woodland, 23, 125, 208, 211
woodland ground covers, 105
woodland phlox, 105, 211
woodland tidytips, 194
woodland tulips, 141

Xanthorhiza simplicissima, 108

yarrow, 180
yellow floating heart, 83
yellow-flowered acacia, 220
yellow foxglove, 132
yellow pitcher plants, 85
yellow root, 108
yellow wax bells, 103, 106
yews, 121, 136, 137
Yucca filamentosa, 78
yuccas, 78, 179, 180

Zea mays 'Japanese Variegated', 75
zinnias, 179
Zizia aptera, 262
zonal geraniums, 188

1 Front Gate
2 Pergola
3 Lilac Border
4 Flower Garden
5 Marco Polo Stufano Conservatory
6 Paisley Bed
7 Perkins Visitor Center
8 Herb + Dry Gardens
9 T. H. Everett Alpine House
10 Gold Border
11 Kerlin Overlook
12 Wild Garden
13 Wild Garden Gazebo
14 Aquatic Garden
15 Rossbach Monocot Garden
16 Shade Border
17 Wave Hill House
18 Kate French Terrace
19 Back Gate
20 Conifer Slope
21 Herbert + Hyonja Abrons Woodland
22 Woodland Trail
23 Woodland Gazebo
24 Elliptical Garden
25 Glyndor Gallery
26 Glyndor Terrace